This book is a must-read if…

- ◊ you regularly ask yourself these questions:
    - ◊ "Why am I here?"
    - ◊ "Why me?"
    - ◊ "Why did I go through that painful experience?"
- ◊ you are ready to go on a journey of discovery
- ◊ you wish to find your purpose in life
- ◊ you want to turn around painful experiences that you have gone through
- ◊ you desire to pursue your purpose
- ◊ you are looking for something to guide you
- ◊ you are pondering on your gifts and what to do with them
- ◊ you are seeking help to make sense of situations that may seem senseless or too painful to bear.

Ihuaku P. Nweke is on a mission to deliver tools and strategies that will enable you to discover your unique gifts and turn your passion and pain into purpose, creating a fulfilled life.

Praise for Ihuaku P. Nweke

"Ihu is a truly remarkable woman who, through walking through the pain and adversity in her own life victoriously, has produced powerful testimonies that not only glorify God, but have identified and excelled in her life purpose and mission. My favourite chapter in her book is Chapter Seven: Keys and Access, which is packed full of powerful nuggets and principles to unlock favour and purpose. Service, sacrifice and obedience are unheard of in today's culture promoting narcissism, rewarding bad behaviour and victimhood.

Ihu's passion and perseverance have been extraordinary in building the ministry she founded, Building the Excellent Family summit that earned her a place in the *World Book of Greatness* and the *New York Times*' Top 30 Women Leaders to Look Out For In 2024. Her endeavour is inspiring and will no doubt have generational impact on the innumerable families transformed by her God-appointed mission."

Wai-Yee Schmidt
Associate of Charles Dombek, Founder of axiumwealth.com

"An insightful, easy-to-read book exploring the role we each have to play in fulfilling our specific purpose on Earth. Backed up by scripture and filled with straightforward illustrations, Nweke delivers a compelling argument that leaves the reader excited to actualise for themselves and for the world all their unique gifting(s)."

Cynthia Tooley MBE
TV Judge of *Great Chocolate Showdown* and Charity Director

"The title of this book says it all: Ihuaku expresses the reality of life, and one cannot detail life as much as she has, if you have not experienced it in the manner she has. Ihuaku, I love your energy, passion and tenacity. You are a real role model.

I admire how Ihuaku has sincerely poured out her heart and used her personal experience to express the need for us to accept challenges, whilst we persevere and allow the process of our purpose for life to materialise. Life is a matter of give and take.

Ihuaku has put a lot of hard work into this book with prayers and biblical quotes in all chapters, thus pointing out how our life is interwoven with the words from different chapters of the Bible, whether you are a Christian or not.

The way she narrates pain before gain resonates with my life story and it affirms my belief, that there is always a bright light at the end of the tunnel. She sees adversity as part of life, a learning curve that enables us to achieve our goal.

Ihuaku demonstrated in so many ways how faith was the muscle that allowed her to walk with confidence, determination and resilience to achieve her purpose for life.

We owe so much to leaders like Ihuaku who has inspired and empowered other women and men in similar situation, and helped them to overcome their difficulties and never to give up hope.

I recommend this book, not only as a book to read, but it is filled with activities at the end of each chapter for individual soul searching, to find your purpose for life."

Cllr Chief Dr Kate Anolue
Author, Freeman of London Borough of Enfield
Former Mayor of London Borough of Enfield

"*The Awakening of Purpose Through Passion and Pain* is a transformative journey that resonates with the depths of the human soul. This book is a powerful testament to the resilience of the human spirit, illustrating how our greatest challenges can ignite our deepest passions and lead us to a life of profound purpose.

With heartfelt stories and insightful wisdom, it serves as both a guide and a companion for anyone seeking to turn their struggles into a source of strength and meaning. A must-read for those yearning to discover their true path."

Professor Chris Imafidon
Guinness Book World Record Holder, Renowned STEM Leader,
UK Platinum Jubilee Education Chair appointed by
the late HRM Queen Elizabeth II

The *Awakening* of Purpose
Through *Passion and Pain*

*For Everyone on a Journey
to Fulfilment*

Ihuaku P. Nweke

BOOK BRILLIANCE
PUBLISHING

First published in Great Britain in 2024
by Book Brilliance Publishing
265A Fir Tree Road, Epsom, Surrey, KT17 3LF
+44 (0)20 8641 5090
www.bookbrilliancepublishing.com
admin@bookbrilliancepublishing.com

© Copyright Ihuaku P. Nweke 2024
All images are copyright of Ihuaku P. Nweke unless specified

Cover art by Joshua Rotimi Adeyemi

The moral right of Ihuaku P. Nweke to be identified as the author of this work has been asserted in accordance with the Copyright, Designs and Patents Acts 1988.

All rights reserved. No part of this publication may be reproduced, stored in a retrieval system, or transmitted, in any form or by any means without the prior written permission of the publisher, nor be otherwise circulated in any form of binding or cover than that in which it is published and without similar condition being imposed on the subsequent purchaser.

A CIP catalogue record for this book is available at the British Library.

ISBN 978-1-913770-82-2.

All biblical references in this book are taken from the New King James Version (NKJV) translation of the Bible.

Dedication

I dedicate this book to the people that have helped shape my past, present and future.

The Past: my father, Dr Obi Nwagwu Chinyere-Ezeh (The Action Doctor). I would not be the woman I am today if it weren't for you. You named me after your mother which means so much to me: Ihuaku, the face of fortune. You told us as you passed away that our names mean so much, and I believe that name is shaping every bit of my fortune today. Your indomitable, optimistic, try-it-all, do-it-all spirit lives on in all your children, and most would agree, it is most evident in me! I know you are always with me. The book you wrote, *The Coup Menace*, left such an impression on me, so much so that I am now authoring mine. You showed me the importance of leading by example and leaving a legacy, so thank you!

The Present: my mother, Geraldine Obi Nwagwu. You are the formidable glue that holds our family together, my number one cheerleader. You are always there, no matter what project I pick up, cheering and supporting. It gives me so much comfort to know you will be there no matter what, so thank you!

The Future: my children, Arinze, Kosi and Chikamso, my pride, hope and joy. When I see the three of you, I have hope for the future and I cannot wait to see what you will all become. I am grateful that God has entrusted me with the responsibility of being a mother to three great, bright and talented young men, and to play a large part in shaping your futures. This is a responsibility I do not take lightly. Thank you to your dear souls for allowing me to do that and for being my teachers as much as I am yours.

Acknowledgements

I would like to acknowledge and thank my husband Chidiebere for being a large part of my story and everything I do, for his part in my projects and his patience, steadfastness and unwavering support, and for lending his critical analysis to many parts of this book.

I acknowledge Brenda Dempsey and the phenomenal Book Brilliance Publishing team for their professionalism, for their patience in bearing with me whilst I authored this book, and for their phenomenal insights that have made sure this book is as polished a product as it can be.

I acknowledge and thank C. Ben Bosah for quickly coming to my rescue and recommending the phenomenal artist Joshua Rotimi Adeyemi to translate my vision for the book cover into reality – thank you!

Contents

Foreword 1

Introduction 3

Part One: Knowing Your Purpose 7

Chapter One: Self-knowledge, Purpose and Passion 9

Chapter Two: Your Passion 25

Chapter Three: Pain 41

Chapter Four: Your Skills 53

Chapter Five: Gifts in Three Parts 65

Chapter Six: Mountains and Mantles 75

Chapter Seven: Keys and Access 85

Part Two: Resourcing Your Purpose 101

Chapter Eight: Assign Your Time, Appoint Your Life 103

Chapter Nine: Your Purpose Needs Money 115

Chapter Ten: Your Purpose Needs People 121

Chapter Eleven: Single On Purpose 129

Chapter Twelve: The Purpose-Aligned Marriage .. 137

Chapter Thirteen: Developing Purpose
in Children 143

Chapter Fourteen: Overcoming Satanic
Opposition – My Story 149

Chapter Fifteen: Conclusion: The Purpose in
the Passion and Pain 163

References and Further Reading 169

Special Thanks 175

About the Author 177

Foreword

In a world filled with endless possibilities and challenges, the journey of awakening one's purpose is a sacred and transformative odyssey. It is a path illuminated by both the radiant light of passion and the profound lessons of pain. The pages you are about to delve into offer a map to navigate this extraordinary terrain.

Within Ihu's words, you'll discover the essence of purpose – a beacon that draws us closer to our true selves. Through passion, we find the unbridled energy that fuels our souls, and through pain, we unearth the hidden gems of wisdom that ultimately guide us to our higher calling.

As I reflect on the pages of this book, I'm reminded of the age-old saying that it's often in the darkest of nights that we see the brightest stars. This book shines a light on the importance of embracing both our joys and sorrows, our victories and defeats, for they are the threads that weave the fabric of our unique purpose.

Ihu's profound insights and heartfelt stories take you on a journey of self-discovery, encouraging you to explore your passions, confront your pains, and transmute them to something that becomes not only beneficial to you, but shines a light on a world that so needs it. In doing so, it unlocks the door to a purpose that transcends the ordinary. It is my sincere hope that as you read these pages, you will feel a deep resonance with the wisdom within and find the inspiration to embark on your true path to awakening purpose.

May this book be your trusted guide, as you set forth on this extraordinary quest. With an open heart and a willingness to embrace all that life offers, you are on the cusp of a remarkable transformation.

Remember, it is through passion and pain that we awaken to the purpose that has been calling us all along.

Dame Marie Diamond

Transformational leader, six times global bestselling author, and star of "The Secret".

www.mariediamond.com

Introduction

The Awakening of Purpose Through Passion and Pain is for everyone who has ever asked themselves, "Why am I here? Why me? Why did I go through that painful experience?"

The book is designed to:

- ◊ Take you on a journey of discovery
- ◊ Draw out your purpose in life
- ◊ Turn around painful experiences that you have gone through
- ◊ Pursue your purpose and help others make sense of situations that may seem senseless or too painful to bear.

I am on a mission to deliver some tools and strategies that will enable you to discover your unique gifts and turn your passion and pain into purpose, creating a fulfilled life.

I was led to write this book by divine inspiration; that we have all come to this world for a purpose. The variety of human personalities, preferences, predispositions, and experiences are far too unique and at the same time universal not to be by a greater design and for a higher purpose.

Having a deep-rooted faith and love of God, as well as a deep connection to my own purpose, I believe that this book will have a broad appeal to all people of all or no faiths. The intention, while referencing biblical stories, is to explain the metaphorical meaning so that we all understand the messages and power of love, faith and hope.

I hope that my book will contribute to building a global community of awakened, purpose-driven individuals, who are using their gifts and redefining their painful experiences to transform themselves and others and, in turn, the world we all live in.

This is important to me because I feel that each human soul has a precious gift to give. The sooner this gift is discovered, the less pain will be endured in searching for it. Consequently, more precious lives would be saved from living without meaning, being directionless, and having destitute existences. My vision is for us all to ultimately become awakened, happier members of humanity.

The Awakening of Purpose Through Passion and Pain has religious undertones with a generous smattering of biblical references and quotes as well as circular, cultural, historical and scientific references that all can relate to. The Christian Bible is my reference point and even though you may not be religious in any shape or form, most of you will resonate with the universal wisdom, narrative and stories contained in the Bible.

This book incorporates my experiences, experiences of well-known personalities, as well as those of people I interviewed in the course of the book to garner the power of self-knowledge, passion and purpose. Many of us seek a higher purpose of some sort, be it via religion, spirituality or other means.

You will also find threads which resonate with my values: Creativity built on inspiration, intuition and innovation; Integrity built on truth, honesty and trust; and finally, Courage built on conviction, determination and vision.

I hope you enjoy reading *The Awakening of Purpose Through Passion and Pain*.

Ihuaku P. Nweke

Part One

Knowing Your Purpose

Chapter One
Self-knowledge, Purpose and Passion

"All things were created by him, and for him."

(Colossians 1:16)

What is the meaning of purpose? This is the one question that has captivated humanity since time immemorial. The *Oxford English Dictionary* definition of purpose is:

the reason for which something is done or created, or for which something exists

Humanity has always wanted to know the reason for its existence. There is, and always has been, so much talk about purpose. However, many people in their forties, fifties, and sixties still don't know what their life's purpose is – indeed, many never discover it.

Many leaders today have outlined their definitions of purpose through various interviews and publications.

Author Bob Proctor simply said, "Purpose is what we love to do." And Oprah Winfrey's purpose is "To be a teacher. And to be known for inspiring my students to be more than they thought they could be."

Another apt description of purpose is given by the well-known author and speaker on leadership, John C. Maxwell, who describes purpose as "How you use your experiences, talents, and passions to better the lives of those around you."

For me, your purpose is your life's work and the reason for your existence, doing what you were created to do. The innate talents that we are born with – our natural passions, preferences and inclinations – all point towards our purpose. Our life experiences – the ups and particularly the downs – indicate how we direct those efforts and talents towards fulfilling our ultimate purpose on earth.

I believe that we are all an expression of the God-source. In Christianity, many believe that the use of our gifts, talents and experiences to the service of humanity, honours God and is a form of worshipping Him. This life-giving source is magnified by showcasing your talents and is glorified when the world benefits from the talents He has gifted you which display His magnificence.

The importance of self-knowledge

I think that most of the problems that you face in life are based on the lack of realisation that you are made in the image of a higher power and can harness this image yourself. Therefore, the situations you find yourself in are consciously or unconsciously created by you. This perspective leads to your acknowledgement that you too are a creator.

Indeed, the Apostle Paul states; *"Do not be conformed to this world but be transformed by the renewing of your mind."* (Romans 12:2)

Once armed with this knowledge, you will know how to respond when you are placed in an environment or situation where you are being treated in the wrong manner. If you lack self-knowledge, you will accept any situation or treatment and feel helpless to change it. It's about knowing your value and how you can enrich the world through your purpose.

Every situation in life is based on your self-image and your concept of who you are. The terms 'Man of God' or 'Woman of God' are religious, rather dogmatic terms because all humans are in effect men and women of God, as we are all made in the likeness of God. Whether or not we realise this truth is another matter.

"So, God created man in His own image, in the image of God He created him; male and female, He created them."

(Genesis 1:27)

Moreover, Daniel says, *"Those who know their God shall be great and do exploits."* (Daniel 11:32)

However, I always wondered whether this was a misinterpretation and whether the correct scripture should have been, "Those who know they're God [in other words, those who are fully convinced of the power and essence of God in themselves] shall be great and do exploits."

Humans are supposed to be the masters of and have dominion over our environment and situations (which includes our works of life), and it is in this mastery that we can show others the way. We are meant to help each other within the specific areas of our 'God domain', and in so doing, we are transformed to become more like the God source in all of us.

The expression of divinity in you is limitless, but it is based on your ability to receive it. You are born with free will which enables you to make choices; choices that support your values and who you are, no matter your circumstances, whether they are adverse or favourable, negative or positive, or entrapping or freeing. Your free will is always in operation and your capacity to receive is based on your level of belief in yourself and the power in you to change your situation or affect that change. In other words, **your faith**.

As Jesus said to Matthew,

> *"Truly I tell you, if you have faith as small as a mustard seed, you can say to this mountain, 'Move from here to there,' and it will move. Nothing will be impossible for you."*
>
> (Matthew 17:20)

Fear limits our faith

Fear, which is the opposite of faith, limits our belief and makes us waiver, over-prepare or procrastinate. We can see this in the Bible when Jesus beckoned Peter to walk on water. Peter could walk on water when he was walking 'in faith', however, as soon as his faith waivered through the onset of fear (i.e. about what he was able to achieve), walking on water became impossible and Peter began to sink.

Fashion is one of my passions and in 2014, I was given a fantastic opportunity as part of a project to bring female black entrepreneurs to the world stage through fashion. I was offered the opportunity to showcase a collection of jewellery at African Fashion Week in London. I had partially started the collection but had yet to complete it. I accepted the offer in faith and decided to work frantically on my collection to complete it on time. The result was that I was catapulted onto the world stage, thus kick-starting my formal fashion design career. Without my faith and acceptance of the offer, I would not have gained recognition and exposure for the work that I loved.

It is impossible to please God without believing in ourselves. Without internal belief, we cannot manifest the potential of our highest power and nature, stretching our faith beyond our perceptions and walking through life in that belief. Choosing to walk with purpose means dwelling in the full expression of your divine beliefs through your thoughts, words and deeds. Faith is not an intellectual exercise and is nothing without good intentions that are backed up by action, because true faith is manifested in what you do and the positive ripples that it produces among people and communities. Faith is the fuel that causes us to act; our thoughts, words and actions are the manifestation of that faith.

The great boxer Muhammad Ali was known for his famous quote, "I am the greatest." In fact, what he said was, "I am the greatest, I said that before I knew I was." He backed up this belief by fighting many of the greatest heavyweight boxers of his time, such as Joe Frazier, and his self-belief proved correct! If he boasted that he was the greatest without ever stepping into the boxing ring, he would have been known as a laughing stock or a dreamer and would never have become the icon that he was. He believed that his status would provide a higher stage to share his purpose – the words and actions of which would bring freedom to many.

1 John 4:18 says *"Perfect love drives out fear"*. If fear is the opposite of faith, then love and faith are synonymous. One cannot love fully with fear. Think of a newborn baby, who is the truest and purest essence of our God-self, who has not been shaped by life experiences; it loves and trusts with no fear.

To deepen your understanding, consider why the scriptures say *"The righteous shall live by faith."* (Galatians 3:11)

The Bible is filled with many metaphors to help you understand its messages. Faith is the oxygen of living our lives in the fullness of our God-like selves, which is predominantly manifested in creativity. Fear stifles this creative power in us.

> *"Faith is the substance of things hoped for,*
> *the evidence of things not yet seen."*
>
> (Hebrews 11:1)

It is easy to strengthen faith when you see and witness the evidence of it. However, having faith in what you cannot or have not yet seen is a testimony to your belief of a higher power. If you can see the full picture and the outcome beforehand, then this is a certainty rather than faith. It is through taking each step and action at a time that the next step or action is revealed.

Now that we have explored the story of Peter walking on water without faith and understood the power of faith, let us revisit the story underpinned with faith. The water was not solid before Peter stepped out of the boat. When Jesus asked him to follow Him and walk on water, Peter put one foot in front of another with faith, and so the water solidified under his feet.

It is by taking one step of obedience after another, such as sitting down at your desk in front of your laptop to write your book, paying for a sewing machine, enrolling in a class to start the fashion business you've been dreaming about for years, or buying a ticket to a conference. Whatever next step you need to take will become apparent on the preceding step, as this is how faith works. Opportunities are presented to you at the divine timing when you are ready to grow in your purpose based on the preceding actions you took through faith.

Serving your purpose brings fulfilment

Most of the time, when you experience a feeling of emptiness, it is because you're not serving your purpose; in other words, you're not living your life as intended. You are not being true to yourself or connected to the values that are the divine source within you.

When a barrel is not full of water, it is empty or partially so, but when it is filled, it is 'full filled' and serving the purpose for which it was made. When you are serving your purpose, you will be filled, and therefore fulfilled! When you are serving your purpose, you can pour your time, treasure and talent out to others because you have filled yourself up, and therefore you have a surplus to give. The more you pour into yourself by investing time and money and learning about what talents and genius you have been given, the more filled you will be and the more time, money and talent you will have to give to others. Understand this: the more you give, the more you receive to continue your work in life.

Creativity is key. Creativity makes us feel alive, gives us joy and attracts beautiful things, people and experiences into our lives, helping us to live life to the full.

When you are creating, you are growing and expanding. When you are living your true purpose, you ignite yourself first and then those in your immediate vicinity will be inspired and galvanised by the strength of your passion and the joy you exude from pursuing it. The whole world benefits from you living the life you were born to live.

Do not get hung up on what you're doing for the rest of your life. If you want to make changes to walk more in line with your purpose, simply start with what you are doing now, because that is the key to shaping your desired future. Consider the following questions:

- What are you doing right now?
- Is it truly what you want to do?
- Whatever you are doing right now, is it helping you achieve your desired future?
- What has not following your purpose cost you in terms of income, connections and fulfilment?
- What are you missing out on?
- What life are you not living because you have not pursued your passions and purpose?
- What life are you not living because you have not done what you are gifted to do, or being who you have been called to be?

The interrelatedness of our purposes

This may sound like sacrilege to many, but the prevalent belief is that all humans are children of God and made in His image. Therefore, we also are infused with our unique expression of the one true God-source within us. We all originate from the one true source of all things.

Given that we come from the one source, it follows that we are all also interrelated. Like links on a chain, we are connected. Your ability to pursue and fulfil your purpose can directly or indirectly help or hinder the ability of another to fulfil theirs.

Similarly, fulfilling your calling and purpose can be dependent on, or greatly enhanced by, someone else fulfilling their purposes. Ultimately, fulfilment is not simply about you but about all of us, as collective members of humanity.

Imagine a world without the light bulb if Thomas Edison had given up on his efforts to invent the carbon filament light bulb at the thousandth try in 1879! But would Edison have even thought this feat possible if Humphry Davy had not invented the electric arc lamp in 1802?

In turn, both of these inventions would not have been possible at all had Benjamin Franklin not discovered the power of electricity in 1752! This is the domino effect, cause and effect in motion. As Isaac Newton said, we stand "on the shoulders of giants." Everyone is interrelated.

Passion

> *"If you have a strong purpose in life,
> you don't have to be pushed.
> Your passion will drive you there."*
>
> Roy T. Bennett, American Thought Leader

I am inspired by Roy T. Bennett as to how to differentiate between passion and purpose; your passion is connected to things and inanimate objects, whilst your purpose is tied to living things. Let me explain further. As mentioned above, I have a passion for design and creativity using the medium of fashion. In addition, I feel that my purpose is to help people discover their own purpose to have healthy relationships and to live fulfilled lives.

I love the Afrobeat musician Tekno, and like all other talented musicians, Tekno's passion is his music. In his pursuit of that passion through diligent practice, application of skill and investment in training, he fulfils his purpose of bringing joy to the world through his music.

Your skills and your passion can lead to the fulfilment of your purpose because your passion for something and the skills you develop in pursuing that passion can bring fulfilment to others. That fulfilment is manifested in the expression of one or more of the nine fruits of the spirit which are love, joy, peace, patience, kindness, faithfulness, gentleness, goodness (generosity) and self-control.

> *"All things work together for good to them that love God,
> to them who are the called according to his purpose."*
>
> (Romans 8:28)

Whenever you are using any gift or talent that the higher power has given you and cultivating it to its fullness, you are magnifying Him. When you magnify God through gratitude and appreciation, it is a form of worship; ultimately, that is what we are born to do: give thanks for our lives.

Imagine a doting father who buys his son a flute for his birthday. The son takes up playing the flute with great passion and enthusiasm, practising daily. He researches several tutorials online to make him an even better player. One day, he composes a beautiful piece and plays it for his father. His father is so proud of his son and feels honoured that he valued the gift he gave him to the extent that he invested time and money to develop it.

One day, the father arranges a dinner party for all his friends. After dinner, as his guests are settling down, he calls his son in to play them the beautiful piece he composed. As his son plays to his friends, the father beams with pride as everyone looks on in admiration, mesmerised by the young man's talent. The performance is followed by rapturous applause and the father is congratulated on having such a talented son who is committed to developing his talent. Everyone benefits from the gift: the father, the son, and everyone who listens to the beautiful music.

This is the same for our God in heaven. He is so proud of us when we are diligent to make the best of our gifts and wants us to display them so that the world can enjoy them too.

Imagine, on the other hand, how the father would feel if his son discarded the flute and left it to gather dust under the bed. If he made no effort to play and practice. This is what our Father feels when we do not use the gifts and talents that He has blessed us with.

We are all the manifestation of different expressions, variations and dimensions of God's magnificence. The Supreme Being loves beauty and variety. All you need to do is listen to the hundreds of different languages spoken by humans around the world and even dialects within each language. Notice the differing beauty and fragrance of a lily to that of a rose, or take in the sight and fragrant beauty of a lavender field to know this is true. Look at the different breeds of animals. Look at the different variations of colours of birds in the sky, and fish and sea life. Each bird in the sky and fish in the sea has its specific characteristics and purpose.

Our passions – what we love to do or the different forms of expression that we are drawn to – are indicators of the unique expression of the higher power within us. When we pursue and cultivate these passions, the result is usually the highest expression of our divinity on earth.

You can see this repeated time and time again in history. Think of artists such as Michelangelo and Leonardo da Vinci, or composers such as Mozart and Beethoven. Think of the musical artists such as Michael Jackson. Think of the sportsmen and women such as Serena and Venus Williams, and the great footballers Diego Maradona and Pele. Think of scientists such as Einstein, Galileo and Marie Curie.

These great men and women pursued their passions in art, music, sports and science with a singular focus, and as a result, they gained great admiration, fame and financial rewards. In addition, their names will forever be reference points for greatness and can never be erased from the history books of human achievement.

When we use our passions and talents, we will gain success and leave a legacy, including lasting fame, because *"The blessing of the Lord, makes one rich, and He adds no sorrow with it."* (Proverbs 10:22)

By cultivating your passions, you also gain a deep sense of confidence and fulfilment which has great rewards.

It is without doubt that self-knowledge is fundamental to your inner connection to yourself and God. The inner journey is the most fascinating and enlightening journey you can embark on. Being aware of who you are can lead to arousing curiosity about your passion and understanding why you feel so driven about certain topics. The more you know yourself, the more confident you feel in your everyday life.

Being aware of your passion that may have been apparent since your childhood often leads to finding your purpose. As you travel through life, you have encountered both negative and positive situations, and the most important aspect of that is the learning that takes place within that process. Over time, you are enlightened as to why God put you on this Earth; to spread His love through your work and your purpose. When you find this purpose, life takes on a new meaning. With your new-found self-knowledge, you become more powerful to create change in yourself, others and the world.

Prayers

- ◊ *"Oh God thank you for saving me and calling me with a holy calling, not according to my works, but according to Your own purpose and grace which was given to me in Christ Jesus before time began."* (2 Timothy 1:9)

- ◊ *"Oh God, grant me according to my heart's desire and fulfil all my purpose."* (Psalm 20:4)

- ◊ *"Oh God, even though there are many plans in my heart, I pray that nevertheless your Counsel for my life Oh Lord will stand."* (Proverbs 19:21)

Ihu's Proclamations

- ◊ *All things work together for my good because I love God and I am called according to His Purpose. (Romans 8:28)*

- ◊ *Through my union with Christ I too have been claimed by God as His own inheritance. Before I was even born, He gave my destiny; that I would fulfil the plan of God who always accomplishes every purpose and plan in His heart. (Ephesians 1:11)*

Ihu's Reflections

Buy yourself a beautiful journal to write down your ideas and thoughts on my Reflections. Learn to ask yourself deep questions that reveal the real you.

Self-Knowledge

- ◊ Consider what you loved to do as a child.
- ◊ Do you still do it today? If not, why not?
- ◊ What do people compliment you for and what do you do with ease?

Passion

- ◊ Make a list of all the things you love to do.

Purpose

- ◊ If you had a magic wand, what would your life look like today?
- ◊ Envision it and write it in your journal.

Stories

- ◊ Think of a time in your life that was challenging.
- ◊ How did you overcome it?
- ◊ How did it make you feel?
- ◊ What lessons did you learn about yourself?

Chapter Two
Your Passion

"For the kingdom of heaven is like a man traveling to a far country, who called his own servants and delivered his goods to them. And to one he gave five talents, to another two, and to another one, to each according to his own ability."

(Matthew 25:14-15)

Your soul's mission drives your passion. What is your passion? For me, passion is a deep feeling of love that inspires action. Most people associate passion with the love of a vocation, an interest or a person. Much has been said about doing work that is aligned with your passion. Consider the work you do every day; do you do that with passion? People who are passionate about their work focus on the feeling they receive from carrying out the task, the difference they are making, and the value they are adding, even in the absence of monetary reward.

As adults, societal expectations force us to be burdened with the responsibilities of paying bills, putting food on the table, and raising a family. For generations, we have tended to view jobs as a financial solution, often forgetting what brings us joy. What if you turned this perspective on its head and used joy to fuel the passion for your work?

Have you ever wondered why when a baby is born, we talk about "a bundle of joy"? When we watch babies develop into toddlers with their unbridled curiosity, sense of adventure and joy, we smile broadly and our spirits are uplifted. Remember, you were once that fearless bundle of joy as you learnt to walk, ride a bike or swim.

> *"Then Jesus called a little child to Him, set him in the midst of them, and said, 'Assuredly, I say to you, unless you are converted and become as little children, you will by no means enter the kingdom of heaven.'"*
>
> (Matthew 18:24)

Let's go back to childhood.

Think back to when you were five, seven, or ten years old. What did you enjoy doing to the extent that you didn't need coercing or encouragement to do it? Perhaps you became so engrossed in that thing that your parents had to plead with you to pause for a short while so that you could focus on other pressing activities.

When you envision these reflections in your mind's eye and engage in the feelings associated with them, it reignites the passion within. Give yourself permission to find the courage you need to revisit your childhood, for therein lies your true soul's passion.

Your passion is your true calling and stands firm in the face of fads, trends and time.

Sometimes, people dissipate their energies moving from one new money-making activity to the other, perhaps in search of a short cut to riches. It could be argued that this stems from an entitlement mentality that is a feature of modern thinking. Many lack the patience to persevere because the path of perseverance through difficulties is challenging and takes time and effort.

These bad habits develop because people have become disconnected from their passion which is buried deep within their subconscious minds. They are derailed and as a result, their true calling and fulfilment of purpose is delayed or, worse still, forgotten about and missed entirely.

Passion is not about doing a million different things; it's about doing the one thing that makes your soul dance. Your passion may not necessarily bring you huge financial rewards, but it will bring you joy, and that is the key to awakening your purpose. Therefore, to find your purpose, it is advisable to follow the feeling of joy.

What is the one thing that you do that brings you the greatest joy?

Many people miss this point and they chase after money, remaining in jobs that are destroying the very essence of their souls. There is nothing wrong with working in a job that does not bring satisfaction, as long as you acknowledge the purpose of that job and that it is a means of achieving a greater purpose, which is part of a grand design. If you acknowledge the role of everything you are doing to fulfil your ultimate purpose, you will not be miserable or downcast in doing what is required to get you there, including working for someone else. The very thought that the job is bringing you closer to your ultimate goal, should itself illicit feelings of joy. Being unhappy in your job could then be an indicator that you have not yet discovered your purpose, are neglecting it, or have not yet mapped out the role that your current job is playing in your purpose.

In the course of writing this book, I interviewed several women, including Heather Picken, who is an NLP business coach, based in Las Vegas. I asked Heather about the one thing in her life that caused her pain or sparked a passion and at the same time changed the trajectory of her life for the better. She explained that as a result of thinking she was fat from the tender age of four years old, she developed anorexia. However, her life changed when she met her partner who is a bodybuilder. She became inspired to become a bodybuilder when she saw how fit, toned and healthy female bodybuilders looked.

She said:

> "There is an amazing connection that happens between decision and discipline that makes you able to achieve."

Heather told me that she went on to have great success in creating a service-based product from what she learned when she decided to pursue bodybuilding as a passion. That passion fuelled her to go through the discipline and rigour required to be a bodybuilder, and this fuelled her further to develop products to help others.

> "When you seem to be sabotaging yourself, such as when you're working in a job that you don't want to be in, what helped when I was in that position was to go through a process of rebalancing the brain which made me think of the positive connections of what I was doing. When your brain comes into balance, the subconscious mind, which forms 95% of your

thinking, will kick into play. It is not something that is forever out of your will; there is force and flow, and we have to be on the side of flow."

Heather's story illustrates how important it is to consistently practice and develop skills in the area of your passion; the love for it will make you persevere through the challenging times that will surely come and will cause you to achieve true mastery in it, as Heather did. The achievement of true mastery leads to being in demand in your field which more than likely leads to financial rewards, acknowledgment or both. Isn't it all the sweeter then, to achieve true mastery in doing what you love?

So do the job, yes, because the bills need to be paid and food needs to be put on the table. However, also make some time to consistently develop skills in the area of your passion; do not neglect or forget your passion whilst you are busy attending to the issues of life.

We may never know the true cost of not pursuing our soul's purpose and passion because sadly, this phenomenon is suffered by approximately 90% of the population of the human race.

In his international bestselling book, *The Body Keeps the Score*, Bessel van der Kolk outlines the effects on the brain, mind and body of trauma. However, I would go deeper and say that not only does the body keep the score, but the soul also keeps the score through lack of direction, disappointment and unfulfillment. Research has proven that between 60% to 80% of primary care visits are due to stress (Nerurkar et al, 2013). A psychosomatic illness occurs when you disconnect from your soul or spirit's essence. If the spiritual or emotional disconnection that triggered the disease is treated, the illness will be healed.

Furthermore, medical research has shown that diseases such as fibromyalgia, depression and anxiety are often triggered by stressful events, including physical, emotional or psychological stress sustained over time. Being out of alignment with what your heart truly wants can cause such stress. These physical manifestations of sickness may be the soul's cry for attention.

Proverbs 13:12 puts it very succinctly: *"Hope deferred makes the heart sick".*

Once the fulfilment of your true heart's desire is deferred, your heart becomes sick and from the heart's sickness comes other sicknesses in the mind, spirit and body.

Solomon, the wise Jewish King, said, *"Keep your heart with all diligence, For out of it spring the issues of life."* (Proverbs 4:23)

I consider that great advice for all of us.

In the end, the soul will keep a score of whether it has succeeded in fulfilling what it set out to do before it was even conceived in physical form.

Multi-passionate

There is nothing wrong with being multi-passionate. This is not the same as being a dabbler and a 'Jack of all trades, master of none', a trait that has received bad press over the ages across all cultures. Is there a possibility, however, that there are some rare humans who possess the ability to master multiple disciplines and passions in their lifetime?

A multi-passionate person, or polymath, is described as "An individual who excels at more than one interest and passion" according to 'The multi-passionate phenomenon' by Dzigbordi K Dosoo in B&FT Online on 4th December 2017. Over the years, some experts have made a distinction between being multi-talented or multi-gifted with the former being identified as inherent traits, whilst being multi-passionate is seen as an acquired skill, a developed strength or generated interest which one pursues with drive and passion.

The Renaissance ideal considered man the centre of the universe, limitless in his capacities for development, which led to the notion that men should try to embrace all knowledge and develop their capacities as fully as possible. Leon Battista Alberti, who lived in Italy from 1404 to 1472, coined this philosophy by saying "A man can do all things if he will."

We can even see this notion echoed in the Bible in Apostle Paul's letter to the Philippians: *"I can do all things through Christ that strengthens me."* (Philippians 4:13)

Indeed, Renaissance men and women were encouraged to master more than one passion. Many of the greatest inventions, works of art, and historical discoveries, were created by Renaissance men and women. Think of Leonardo da Vinci or Michelangelo. Leonardo da Vinci was equally a great architect, sculptor, engineer and draftsman, as well as a painter.

One of America's founding fathers, Benjamin Franklin, was an author, printer, politician and scientist, whose contributions influenced both physics and the invention of electricity.

Nowadays, the term multi-passionate or polymath is being used more regularly, especially for millennials. To an extent, this is thanks to the popular female life coach and speaker, Marie Forleo, herself a polymath.

Shannon Kaiser wrote an article in the *Huffington Post* in 2017, titled '3 Unexpected Ways to Find Your Life Purpose'. In the article, she writes that many of us struggle with trying to find that 'one thing' but that trying to find 'it' is the reason we feel that something is missing. That is to say, the notion that only having one thing we are meant to do limits us from fulfilling our greatness. Shannon – who is a life coach, travel writer, author, speaker and mentor – says that everything she does brings her joy. Her advice is to let go of thinking that a person has only one life purpose, but rather to start getting in touch with your passions; when you live a passionate life, you are living your life on purpose.

Many would call me multi-passionate, and I believe I am indeed a polymath. I have always been creative, ever since I can remember: as a little girl, I sketched beautiful wedding gowns that I had designed myself in my imagination. As I grew older, I acquired skills, qualifications and experience in the field of contracts and procurement. Having now racked up over 20 years of experience in this area, I am considered an expert in this field and have enjoyed financial rewards as a result.

My other passions include family restoration and domestic abuse advocacy. I have a social enterprise called Cedarcube (www.cedarcube.com), which deals with family restoration and through that, I organise many community events both offline and online, as I am also a phenomenal event organiser.

My many interests have seen me contribute to several anthologies and be invited to speak on various national and international platforms.

So, if being multi-passionate is indeed our true state of being, why then is it so frowned upon in the modern age?

In her article, 'What is a Multi Passionate Person? Why The Future Belongs to Multi Potentialites,' Dr Kinga Mnich says that society nowadays is built for and around specialists, people with expertise in one field or skill who build a career around it. This started with industrialisation. The need for developing optimisation processes during the industrial revolution favoured giving each worker one specific task to do.

At the time, this seemed like a great innovation but in modern times, it has been shown to be a major cause of anxiety, depression and the feeling of being unable to fully contribute to society. It is indeed fair to say that mental well-being and a personal sense of purpose were not at the forefront of many companies' thinking during the industrial revolution!

However, there are benefits to both traits; multi-passionate people are often very good at seeing the bigger picture, whilst being a specialist allows one to hone one skill and become the expert or go-to person in that area. It is therefore fair to say that in today's world, there is more than enough room for both multi-passionate people and specialists to co-exist and do so very happily and productively.

The problem is that most people do not have the discipline and drive to successfully develop the right skills they need to excel when they are multi-passionate, so end up with unfinished projects and confusion. This often leaves them unfulfilled, looking and feeling like failures.

Heather Picken advises that being multi-passionate can be a success as long as you put in place the right systems to work on a couple of core issues at a time. However, it is probably wiser to do one thing, get it up to speed so it is the best it can be, then work on another, and so on.

A very successful multimillionaire Chinese businesswoman, Wai-Yee Schmidt, who is also a Bible teacher, whom I interviewed at one of my family summits for Cedarcube, put it this way: "You don't want to go bankrupt in many ways at the same time!"

What to do when you don't know what to do

For many, it is difficult to hone in on that one idea that makes their soul leap and lights their fire. My advice would be to start from the very beginning, and that beginning starts with you! Light the fire in **you** first. Discover what truly lights your fire. When you start using language such as "I have to" and "I must", you are forcing yourself to embark on work that is not truly aligned with your passions or related to an area that you have a passion to solve a problem in. When this happens, you know you are out of alignment with your soul's purpose.

Heather Picken also advises that people who are in the same desolate place that she was before she discovered her passion for bodybuilding, should invest in a coach. If they cannot afford a coach, they should surround themselves with positive people.

> "Get rid of people with a poor mentality, be around people with rich thinking.

"Get off social media, as it encourages comparison and teaches us 'how to think', and get in tune with yourself through journaling and meditating."

Dreams

Dreams are part of our subconscious mind directing us to the right path. When we are in the dream state, our consciousness has reached the theta state of Rapid Eye Movement Sleep (REM) sleep where most dream activity occurs and where the brain frequency oscillates between 4hz and 7hz. This is the same state one enters when in deep meditation or trance, a mindless state if you will. In this state, our mental state is not bogged down by the super awareness of consciousness, but is at its most pure state and closest to its original source. You can call this source 'God' or super consciousness. For the sake of argument, I will call it God.

If you are anything like me, you will often have very clear and vivid dreams in bold technicolour!

Indeed, many inventors received their inspirations through dreams. The modern sewing machine was discovered in this way. In 1845, Elias Howe dreamt that he had been captured by cannibals who gave him an ultimatum; he had to invent a sewing machine in 24 hours or suffer a painful death. He failed so they stabbed him repeatedly with spears that had holes in their tips. This made Howe realise that he had to put an eye on the needle to create the lock-stitch sewing machine he had always struggled to invent.

This is not the only world-changing invention that was shown to the inventor in a dream; the structure of the atom, DNA, Einstein's Theory of Relativity, and even Google, were all discovered in dreams. There is indeed a level of awareness that short-circuits several years of study and is only available in the dream state.

We need to be paying attention to our dreams!

In my dreams, I will often find myself sewing clothes as part of a sewing class or walking into a clothing factory that I own. I even get whole dress designs and ideas given to me in these dreams. I know for sure that this is my soul's calling.

My waking life confirms and bears witness to what my soul has always known, which is that my deepest, purest and truest calling is to express my 'Godself' through the design and creation of beautiful clothes. Though I have a clothing brand called I.Kollection that has been featured in *Vogue* and has received several awards, I know that I have tapped into less than 10% of the full realisation and fulfilment of this passion and purpose. This is because, like everyone else, I have picked up other purposes, other causes, and the skills that go with them.

As already mentioned, I have a social enterprise that deals with family restoration and through that, I organise many community events both online and in person. However, I know deep down that I will never feel truly accomplished and fulfilled until I explore the fullness of my truest and deepest calling and passion.

Distractions

Distractions divert the soul's purpose. In our modern technological age, it is becoming more and more difficult to focus on one's passions and on what matters. It is almost as if we're in a constant battle with ourselves and this trend has fuelled the boom in the self-help industry. *The 5 Second Rule*, *Atomic Habits* and *The One Thing* are all self-help books that have grown into philosophies to help us focus on the one or few ideas that are our most important soul's purposes. Is it any wonder that without such modern-day distractions, great men and women such as Alexander the Great conquered the world by the age of 25 (dead by 32), leaving an unrivalled legacy? Is it any wonder that Jesus Christ completed his whole ministry, one that is the basis of modern-day Christianity, and had fulfilled his soul's purpose on earth by the age of 33? Indeed, He is remembered as the greatest man that ever lived.

Yet many get embroiled in endless activities due to peer pressure and the fear of missing out, letting their mind feed them a false narrative that they must do everything that everyone else is doing, instead of simply listening to their soul.

Interviews with Bill Gates, Steve Jobs and other technology giants reveal that Silicon Valley CEOs are strict with their children's use of technology, an article in *The Independent* reveals. It goes on to say that research has found that an eighth grader's (Year 9 in the UK, 13-to-14-year-olds) risk of depression jumps 25% when they frequently use social media. Children who use their phones for at least three hours per day are much more likely to be suicidal. In 2007, Bill Gates implemented a cap on screen time when his daughter started developing an unhealthy attachment to a video game. He also didn't let his kids get mobile phones until they turned 14; today, the average age of a child getting their first mobile phone is 10 years old.

The late Steve Jobs revealed that he had prohibited his children from using the newly released iPad. "We limit how much technology our kids use at home," Jobs told reporter Nick Bilton in the *New York Times* in 2017.

According to Scholastic, many children's creativity will reach its peak before the age of six, after which it will begin to decline with the onset of formal education. As mentioned, recognising the limited time window to develop this creative muscle while at its apex early in their children's lives, tech giants like Steve Jobs banned technology to allow creativity to develop fully.

I believe that because our creativity stems from within us rather than without, technology only enables what we already have. However, technology is considered to be a means of entertainment and, more often than not, a distraction. If unmanaged, it can prove to be derailing for an adult trying to achieve their life's purpose, let alone a child that is developing into theirs.

It is easy in this modern age to feel like you're not doing enough. But to what end? If all the activity will ultimately lead you away from what your soul loves to do or causes you to arrive at them much later than would otherwise have been the case, then what benefit is it to you or your life's purpose? If the distractions ultimately divert you from your soul's purpose, why pay attention to them in the first place?

No one can bet on a moving target. The soul is heavy and still like a rock, but the mind is like a babbling brook that always rises to the surface. When all the activity of the rushing brook is over, one thing will remain constant and firm, withstanding the test of time and that is the rock. This is the same with your soul.

Prayers

- ◊ *"God help me to use my gifts that differ according to the grace given to me."* (Romans 12:6-8)

- ◊ *"Oh God, may your grace equip me to let my light shine before others, so that they may see my good works and give glory to my Father who is in heaven."* (Matthew 5:16)

Ihu's Proclamations

- ◊ *"I will use my gift to serve others because I am a good steward of God's varied grace: if I speak, I will speak oracles of God, if I serve, I will serve as one who serves by the strength that God supplies in order that in everything you God may be glorified through Jesus Christ. To him belong glory and dominion forever and ever. Amen"* (1 Peter 4:10-11)

Ihu's Reflections:

- ◊ What is the one thing that brings you joy?

- ◊ What is that one thing that your soul always yearns to do? (That is your core. Discover it and build from that foundation; everything else will follow and fall into place.)

- ◊ Consider the work you do every day. Do you do that with passion?

- ◊ Imagine doing work you are passionate about. How will that impact your life and that of others?

Chapter Three
Pain

> *"My brethren, count it all joy when you fall into various trials, knowing that the testing of your faith produces patience. But let patience have its perfect work, that you may be perfect and complete, lacking nothing."*
>
> (James 1:2-4)

Most of us have gone through some sort of struggle in life, some of which may be persistent or recurring. These experiences pushes us to strive to solve those problems as a means of easing the pain. Our pains and burdens are in effect our crosses to bear; just as Jesus carried His cross to die and fulfil His calling and purpose for the greater good, our problems and challenges are often the keys to unlocking our own purpose. Our primary reason for existence is to help others to resolve life's issues and the best way to do this is through our own lived experiences. We are better placed to help others if we have lived through the same experiences; we cannot give what we don't have and we cannot help someone if we have not gone through a similar pain. Because our purpose is about service to others, our pain is not about us, but is qualifying us to be able to serve others.

Romans 8:28-29 illustrates it perfectly:

"And we know that all things work together for good to those who love God, to those who are the called according to His purpose. For whom He foreknew, He also predestined to be conformed to the image of His Son, that He might be the firstborn among many brethren."

Just as by Jesus' stripes we were healed, others will also be healed by the pain we've gone through if we use it to help others.

There is a message in your mess, a ministry in your misery, a testimony in your test. But you need to pass the test first. Just as gold is refined by going through the fire, so also will you be refined through the experiences and adversity you have endured.

Anything worth having in life takes time, labour, patience, and perseverance, be it writing a book, painting a masterpiece, or building the greatest architecture known to humankind. Making a human being takes nine months of carrying a growing heavy load. Birthing that human being takes a great exertion of effort which comes with significant pain; does it mean it is not worth having? Absolutely not; in fact, the pain and effort make the end product all the more precious and this is the same with your pain. It is hard to recreate, and many would not want to go through the same experience. That is why your pain gives you authority; the experience you have undergone confers a certain level of reverence to you, putting you in the position to guide others to navigate through those experiences, helping them avoid going through quite as much pain as you have.

If you are going through a challenge, take comfort in the knowledge that it may well be a life test that will benefit you and others if you overcome it. Overcoming it will give you proven strategies and a blueprint; however, this takes hard work and a lot of effort. What is it in your life that looks like an immovable mountain, and you are put off by the work involved? Try and tackle it because that is what will leave a lasting monument, a legacy that many will admire and benefit from for ages to come.

Some babies will never be born unless you conceive, birth, carry, and nurture them into being. Some people will die in their pain unless you conquer yours and use that experience to help others. So go ahead and take the first step to conceive that baby today, carry it and birth it, albeit in pain.

Your pain gives you authority

Our lives can often be seen as an open book; with each new day, a new page is written, a chapter completed. Each person's story is as unique to them as is their thumbprint. So in effect, we are authoring our own life story as we live and breathe daily, and this makes you an authority of the experiences you have gone through and the master of the struggles you have conquered. Victories are won in battle and in war, warriors are made.

There is a well-known adage that says "What doesn't kill you makes you stronger." Indeed, you become the master of the struggles and pains you have conquered through life. If you are struggling now, know that despite your current struggles and battles, you will emerge a stronger victorious warrior.

> *"Moreover, whom He predestined, these He also called; whom He called, these He also justified; and whom He justified, these He also glorified."*
>
> (Romans 8:30)

It is true also that the place of your greatest pain will be the place of your sweetest victory. The victory is sweeter when the battle has been the hardest.

At the end of the adversity, you have a clearer insight into who you are, and what your purpose is. Furthermore, you have dug deep to build up a stockpile of resilience, self-reliance and experience, with the knowledge that no matter what, you will survive and rise from the ashes a more magnificent being that reflects more of God's glory and his own image of you rather than what the world expects. You walk more sure-footed on the path that has been chosen for you since the beginning of time.

We previously talked about the pain experienced from not pursuing your purpose and how that can manifest itself in various psychosomatic illnesses. Illnesses can also manifest from traumatic experiences.

Jenny Crowe, one of the ladies I interviewed, spoke about the pain she had experienced from unresolved trauma.

> "I had pain on all levels: physical, mental, emotional, spiritual. I spent 20 years with extreme digestive pain and allergies. There were times when I couldn't eat and was eating baby food because of the trauma that I experienced at a young age. What I learnt from that was that unresolved issues and trauma leading to physical pain can continue into adulthood and haunt your life. I had unresolved trauma which manifested

in gut pain; I could only eat certain foodstuffs, I had irritable bowel syndrome, and I had my gall bladder taken out. I was a mess, and couldn't take any kind of pain medicine at all."

She added, "I was forced to be conscious by my pain and that meant looking for other ways of dealing with pain, and being 'in it'. Being able to endure the pain taught me that the body is a miracle and, amazingly, we can live through the pain and still be okay. I never went to the doctor or was on Intravenous (IV) drip, nutritional supplements or any of that kind of stuff when I lost a lot of weight. I got down to about 103 pounds.

"I was tiny and I couldn't gain weight, and then of course there's all that rejection you get from people who would comment, 'Oh, you're so skinny, oh, you're so sickly,' whereas I would never say, 'You're so fat.' I was trying to save my life and it was very scary because I didn't understand; I was living with the same concepts and beliefs that everything was based on the physical body dimension we could see – I didn't have a full perspective yet. Later, there was also the mental, spiritual and emotional pain, as well as the anguish, and I could go into chapters on each aspect! I've experienced all of the emotional pain; I had a lot of loss over 14 years. Everything started getting taken away from me in my life; it was like seven years of bad luck times two."

Though extremely painful as we have seen, Jenny's experience transitioned her into the journey of stepping into her own purpose as a healer and teacher, a journey also laced with its own pains and challenges.

"As a result of some of the early lessons I learnt which stuck with me through my whole process, I was learning what a good teacher is. I was working with many different 'masters' and would get to a certain level with each one then hit a wall because I would start questioning beyond their limit of understanding and they couldn't handle it. They would stop me and try and knock me down because I wanted to keep going! That's usually when I stopped working with that 'master' because they wanted to control my free will and growth and discredit me, as I was going beyond the limits of what they knew.

"I identified it as sorrow; it was so sad because what I had learned about teachers is that a good teacher learns from their students as well. When you teach, you learn by the reflections and feedback you receive. When I was younger, I had such an idealistic mind about how the world was and should be and at the time, it wasn't going as I expected so I kept saying, 'What do you mean it's not like that?' and the reply was always, 'It's not.' I was so naïve, so when I studied with the 'masters', I understood that many weren't great after all; there were many egos which would get in the way, masking their continued growth and their 'spiritual contracts'. This meant that when we got into a place where there was push back, I knew it was a gift for me as it pushed me on my way to mapping my own way and walking in my own purpose."

Jenny's experiences are unique to her, but we all have our own stories of pain that have shaped the path to our purpose. For many, their painful experience is tied to a relationship with a significant other. Most young girls dream of living a life happily ever after with a Prince Charming who is chivalrous, kind, gentle, and loving. Sadly, for many, the reality of that dream is a nightmare that proves to be the exact opposite of the dream they had envisioned.

Michelle Watson is a coach from London who endured an abusive marriage and has since shaped her purpose in encouraging others to share their stories through writing.

Michelle shares some of her story here:

> "After I got married, things were fine and then I started seeing a lot of changes, particularly when I got pregnant. My husband would become upset if he came home and a member of my family was visiting and he didn't know about it, or if I had gone to visit a member of my family. I noted all these little things but thought it would pass.
>
> "When I was pregnant, he wouldn't allow me to leave the house. He would promise to bring back something for us to eat and I would be starving for the whole day, as he often wouldn't get back until maybe 10 or 11 pm. He would get angry for nothing at all, but because I was having a difficult pregnancy, I didn't have the strength to argue, so I bided my time. However, after I had the baby, it continued.
>
> "I'll never forget one day when we were in a massive supermarket in front of the cashier, and I got a barrage of abuse with words such as 'dog' and other terms. This verbal abuse soon became physical abuse. It reached a point where I would claim any overtime simply to be at work. When I was in the house, I was not allowed to go out even if we needed stuff. He would promise that we would go shopping when he came back. But then he would finish work, visit a friend and not come

home until late. So once again, items weren't bought that we needed.

"Our flat was in a house that had been split into flats, so my neighbours across the way from me obviously realised something was going on. My neighbour's daughter and I were pregnant at the same time and when her mother cooked, she would bring food over for me as she realised how hungry I was. We're still friends to this day!

"The situation was getting worse; I kept making excuses for him and I didn't tell my family. It got to the point where I realised that I had lost who I was. Then I was diagnosed with a tumour... I was told that the left side of my face was going to be paralysed and I felt like digging a hole, one of the darkest holes that you could ever be in, and remaining there. So I say to you, if you see somebody that wishes to take their own life, it's not because they're being selfish. You have no idea of the type of hole they find themselves in and what's festering in their lives. When things fester, you list to yourself all the reasons why it would be better if you were dead because you have no hope and cannot see any way out of it or any point in staying alive.

"I started sleeping in a different room and sometimes, I would wake up and find him standing over me – that would frighten the life out of me. He also locked me in the house and I had to climb through the window to escape. Another time, I was on the phone with my aunt and something happened and she heard the whole episode. She came around because she didn't live far away. We had fought and this time was the first time I fought back. He had poured food all over me and kicked me and something switched and I thought, 'Nah, I am not taking this anymore.'

"I was very ashamed that my aunt witnessed what had happened. I had to beg her not to say anything because I had a cousin who was very boisterous and protective, and I didn't want my husband to get in trouble with him.

"My husband left but then returned and that is when I feared for my life. I decided that being somewhere else was safer, so I started sleeping at a friend's house.

"One night, I heard my husband talking on the phone to a friend and listened to all the lies he was saying about me. I remember sitting in the bathroom thinking, 'Michelle, is this really you?' I began to reflect on my teenage years when I used to debate and was made Head Girl and everything leading up to that point. I thought, 'How did I get here?' And I said to myself, 'You know what? You're the one that got yourself into this and you're the only one that can get you out.' The most painful thing was thinking about my kids; I felt terrible that I was separating them from their dad. This was the last thread I could hold on to but then I realised that I couldn't be a parent to them if I stayed in this toxic relationship.

"And that was the breaking moment. My cousin eventually found out and came to my friend's house to see what was going on. He told me, 'No, Michelle, you need to get out of this relationship.'

"He asked my husband to leave. He refused, so we got the police involved and that was how he left. That's how I got out."

Jenny and Michelle's stories of pain are not uncommon to the human experience. Life is full of its ups and downs, challenges and victories. If we don't give up, we will certainly emerge stronger and equipped to face these challenges and will become a beacon of light and hope to others, showing that it is possible to come out alive on the other side.

The pains of life are there to help define us and make us stronger and wiser.

Prayers

David the embattled king penned several prayers of deliverance. You can research and pray these when in need, but here are snippets that can help you when you need to pray in times of pain and suffering.

> "Oh God, My times are in Your hand; Deliver me from the hand of my enemies, And from those who persecute me."
>
> (Psalm 31:15)

> "Preserve me, O God, for in You I put my trust. I will bless the Lord who has given me counsel; My heart also instructs me in the night seasons. I have set the Lord always before me; Because He is at my right hand I shall not be moved."
>
> (Psalm 16)

Ihu's Proclamations

- *"All things work together for good for me because I am called according to God's purpose."* (Romans 8:28)
- *"I will not be afraid, I will stand still and see the salvation of the Lord, which He will accomplish for me today, For the Egyptians whom I see today, I shall see again no more forever."* (Exodus 14)
- *"The Lord will fight for me, I shall hold my peace."* (Exodus 14)
- *"The waters of my Red Sea now part and I now walk over to my promised land."* (Exodus 14:21-22)
- *I am divinely led – I follow the right fork on the road, God makes a way where there is no way.*
- *I expect the unexpected, my glorious good now comes to pass.*

Ihu's Reflections

- What is it in your life that looks like an immovable mountain, and you are put off by the work involved? (Try and tackle it because that is what will leave a lasting monument, a legacy that many will admire and benefit from for ages to come.)
- What have you learnt from the painful experiences you have endured in life?
- What problems has your pain qualified you to solve?
- Who has your pain qualified you to help?

Chapter Four
Your Skills

"He has filled them with skill to do all manner of work of the engraver and the designer and the tapestry maker, in blue, purple, and scarlet thread, and fine linen, and of the weaver – those who do every work and those who design artistic works."

(Exodus 35:35)

The acquisition and development of skills is vital in refining raw talent, your passion and life's painful experiences, subsequently developing mastery into something marketable and presentable to the world.

The acquisition of skills takes diligence, patience and, of course, perseverance. It is in this discipline that many fall short, failing to develop their passions and experiences into something extraordinary that can be shared with the world and be developed into a movement that can impact lives and generate income.

Skills acquisition is probably the most valuable component of human advancement. Frankly, without the development of skills to underpin grand visions and dreams, the best examples of human progress we have seen to date would remain but mere dreams; there would be no sewing machines, no light bulbs, no cars, and certainly no space travel! The greatest books would not be written, the greatest art masterpieces would not materialise into finished works, and the greatest examples of architecture would not stand but simply exist in the artist's head.

Going back to biblical references, Solomon would not have materialised the grand temple into reality, Noah would not have built that ark and would have drowned with the rest of humanity, and even the Bible itself would never have been written.

Skills are the vehicle that we use to bring our visions and dreams from heaven into earthly reality, "bringing thy will on earth as it is in heaven", as it were. Our visions and dreams are for the ethereal whereas skills belong firmly to flesh and blood in this earthly realm. Every human must acquire a skill or several skills to function and to thrive on this sphere.

In many societies, apprenticeships were a rite of passage from adolescence to adulthood and were found in diverse crafts such as printing, candle-making, dressmaking and millinery. From medieval times, individuals from certain crafts (also known as a 'mystery') began to form craft guilds as a way of ensuring that a certain level of quality was maintained within their craft. There were craft guilds for barbers, cordwainers (shoemakers), bakers, goldsmiths and carpenters, to name a few. Guild members made apprenticeships a requirement for anyone who wished to join them, and those who became master craftsmen in their towns had the right to hire apprenticeships. In 1563, the Great Statute of Artificers was introduced by the government, legislating that anyone who wished to join a craft of their choice would spend no less than seven years as an apprentice in that craft. After this time of service, if they were able to apply themselves in their studies and training, they would then have to serve a further two years to earn the right of working as a journeyman, serving any master of their choice as a paid worker. After this additional two years of service, they could then apply to be recognised as a 'master' of their craft, thus being able to take on their own apprentices and journeymen. (Reading The Past with Dr Kat.)

I am from the Igbo tribe which has now become the most successful ethnic group in Africa. The Igbos are renowned for their business acumen and many attribute the success of the Igbos to the system of apprenticeships, where a businessman or woman takes on an apprentice often from their kindred, to train up in their craft. Akin to the English system, the apprentice would serve a period of six to seven years with their master until they are 'settled' financially or in kind in their own similar business. Following settlement, they can start their own business and possibly train up one or several people in that trade thus propagating businesses across the landscape. This same system of developing skills over knowledge can be seen across various other societies worldwide.

The process of skills acquisition can be illustrated scientifically in what is known as the 'Four Steps to Skill Acquisition'. (Annie Strauch, Performance Medicine)

Neuroplasticity is the term for the brain's ability to reorganise and create neural connections as it processes new information. This process occurs throughout our lifetime, though it may slow down a little with age. The brain may be compared to a muscle which needs to be exercised like the rest of the body to make these neural connections. The more repetitions of the exercise that occur, the stronger the brain gets and the more connections are made. This process is a crucial factor in learning a new skill or modifying a bad habit and forming a better one. When you learn a new skill or change a bad habit, you must undergo the following four steps before it is integrated into your body and ultimately, your way of being or habit.

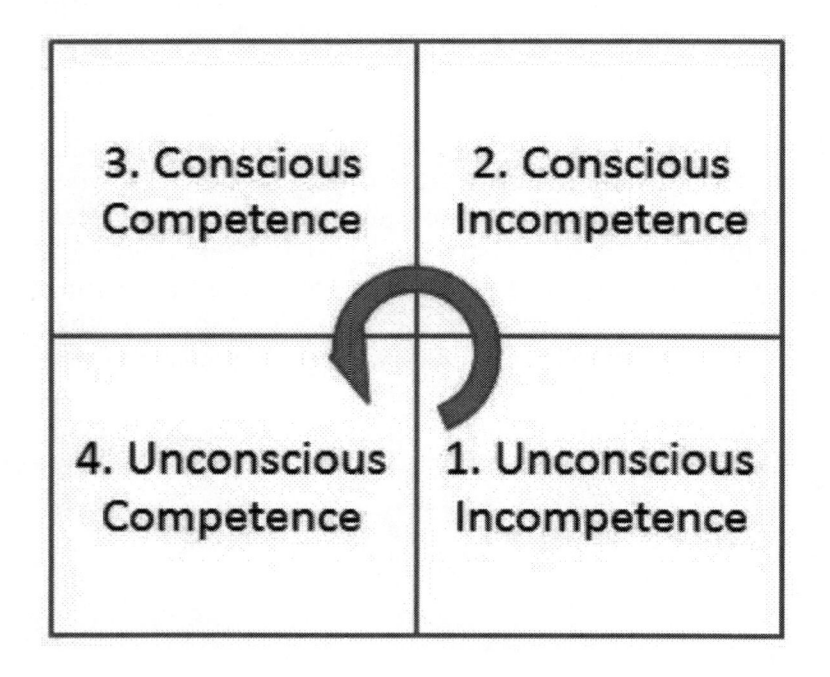

3. Conscious Competence	2. Conscious Incompetence
4. Unconscious Competence	1. Unconscious Incompetence

1. **Unconscious Incompetence.** When you don't know what you're doing or unaware that you're doing something wrong.

2. **Conscious Incompetence.** When you are aware of the bad habit you are trying to get rid of or the skill you want to acquire.

3. **Conscious Competence.** When you are performing the new skill or habit, but with some conscious effort.

4. **Unconscious Competence.** When the new skill or habit becomes integrated into your daily life and routine and the effort now becomes unconscious.

The progression from Step 3 to Step 4 can be the most challenging as you are forming new neural connections and establishing new patterns. Practice and repetition is the best way to integrate a new skill; there is therefore truth in the saying that practice makes perfect. However, we must be certain that we are learning the best method of acquiring those skills, to ensure that we are not learning bad habits and methods in our quest for skills acquisition. Therefore, even better than practice makes perfect is "perfect practice makes perfect" or as my late friend Dr Philip Chan (known as 'The 10-Seconds Maths Expert' in the world) would say, "Perfect practice makes improvement"!

Skills usually fall into one of two categories: soft skills and hard skills. Here are some examples:

Hard skills

- ◊ Coding
- ◊ Editing
- ◊ Tutoring
- ◊ Sewing
- ◊ Financial budgeting and forecasting

Soft skills

- ◊ Confidence
- ◊ Presentation skills
- ◊ Public speaking
- ◊ Focus
- ◊ Teamwork

Values often are natural attributes but like every other skill, they can be learnt. They help in developing emotional and social intelligence which aid navigating through life and achieving success in our purpose. Some skills that are also considered values are outlined below:

Values

- ◊ Empathy
- ◊ Kindness
- ◊ Consideration
- ◊ Humility
- ◊ Integrity
- ◊ Honesty
- ◊ Self-discipline
- ◊ Focus

Evidently we must acquire skills and life would be most simple and enjoyable if we acquired those skills primarily in the areas of our passions. Sadly, this does not often happen.

What usually happens is that the pressures of life push us in one direction, often away from our natural talents and gifts, forcing us to develop skills in an area or areas that are completely misaligned with our natural inclinations. By the time we realise this, it is too late because bills must be paid, the children need to be fed, and we must show up at work. In short, the pressures of life take over. Despite being armed with the knowledge that their jobs are misaligned with their true selves, most people do not have the time or energy after a full day's work to make the necessary investments required to develop their passions – I think this is a crying shame.

At this stage, it would take a Herculean effort to go through the aforementioned stages of competence necessary to achieve mastery and develop the skills in the specified area of passion. However, with some discipline and determination, it can be done.

Your skills can be used to earn a living to then fund your passion and pain, and in turn funding your purpose. As previously mentioned, I have always been creative and as a young girl, I sketched designs of wedding and dinner dresses on paper, imagining what they would look like if they were translated into reality.

However, my career path took a different turn because coming from an African heritage, I assumed that my parents would not want me to pursue a career in a creative field which was seen as less desirable than pursuing a more academic-based profession such as medicine, engineering or law. I ended up studying economics at university, subsequently pursuing a Master's degree in Business Information Technology. I found myself as an HTML coder at the BBC, which wasn't a bad first job after university!

Following my short stint there, I landed what would be termed as a very "good job" with the renowned advertising firm Ogilvy & Mather in their interactive advertising department, Ogilvy Interactive. I lived the glamorous life of an ad agency girl, with a swanky office in Cabot Square in London's prestigious Canary Wharf and one on Regent Street's north side, known as 'Noho'. Monthly parties including summer boat parties, free coffee and fruit at work were the norm. That was until the 'dot com' bubble bust, and we were all made redundant in the millennium crash of the year 2000.

I got a reasonably handsome pay out for a 22-year-old, £3,500. As I couldn't find another job in the technology space, I ended up working for my father, helping him to win new business for his healthcare agency. In addition, my mother paid for me to learn jewellery making and I would attend classes at weekends. The job with my dad lasted for about a year then I took on other odd jobs, such as a customer service agent and a call centre researcher.

Around that time, I started Cedarcube, which was geared towards helping Christian singles find an avenue for entertainment without having to frequent secular nightclubs. In the course of this research, I met my husband Chidi (I will tell this story later!).

My husband (then boyfriend) persuaded me to look for a better job in the local authority and that led me to my first procurement job at the London Borough of Tower Hamlets. Seemingly by accident, these set of occurrences kick-started my now 20-year procurement career.

I have developed my skills within procurement which included obtaining a professional qualification involving studying and passing 15 exams, five at each level. All in all, my training in procurement took four years and resulted in my obtaining chartered status. The learning continues as I rack up more years of experience in different sectors, such as local and central government, healthcare and pharmaceuticals. Through this training, I have become proficient and a master in the profession and have become well-rewarded, as such financially. The financial rewards have been beneficial in helping take care of my family, as well as funding my passion and my mission to help others through the lessons learnt from my pain.

The benefits of skills acquisition

1. **You increase your value:** The more you develop yourself, the more your value proposition increases and the more you have to offer the world.

    For instance, being skilled in procurement also helped me become a better buyer and negotiator in everything else I did.

2. **Financial stability:** The more your value increases, the more you can help others and the more you earn.

    When I didn't work for almost two years, it was the skills I had in designing and making clothes and procuring fabric for my fashion business, that softened the financial blow for me and my family.

3. **Freedom to make more choices:** You can choose to work a nine-to-five job or to start your own business.

4. **Independence:** Skills acquisition helps you not to rely on others. When you become skilled at what you do, you are in charge of your own economy

and do not have to depend on others for your upkeep. In fact, if you really focus on developing your skills, you may one day be the one supporting and helping others.

5. **Self-confidence:** Acquiring and mastering skills helps to build unshakable self-confidence. When you have capabilities and you can create something with your knowledge and hands, it builds self-confidence that will open doors of opportunity for you.

Through my ability to design clothes, I was able to design outfits for Marie Diamond. It led us to develop a relationship and she has now authored the foreword to this book!

Ideally, you should develop skills around your passion; however, as mentioned, life happens. Try and maintain the focus, and identify the purpose of everything you do in your life and work. I enjoy my procurement career; I have become a master in it over the years and have enjoyed the financial benefits it has brought me. However, I understand that this skill is a vehicle for me to fund my purpose and in as much, as it is tempting to settle for a comfortable life earning a great income which procurement can and has offered me, I am determined not to as I know there is more to achieve.

I am very clear and aware that it is not my ultimate purpose but a vehicle to achieve my purpose in the areas of my passion and pain. I still run a fashion brand and work to maintain my skills in that area, perhaps not as rigorously as I should; however, I am not letting the embers of that passion die.

Similarly, I run a charitable organisation, maintaining a mission to help 500 families over five years. Through this vehicle, I have spearheaded initiatives such as fundraising for single mothers and reaching families through an annual summit called Building the Excellent Family.

Is it easy to have all these commitments and interests at once? Absolutely not! However, I am clear of my purpose on Earth, and I am determined to fulfil it. Of course, it would be easier for me to settle in a nine-to-five job and make money, go on lovely holidays every year and simply be comfortable, but to me, that would not be fulfilling my purpose.

This is where many people get stuck: they start off with a great purpose, a passion which shows itself when they are a child, then they are encouraged to get a good job. The money is attractive. Then life happens: they get married, get a mortgage, and have children. Bills must be paid and the family maintained, and this is where the dreams die.

If we put in perspective, the scientific fact that you are one of nine billion unique humans on Earth who have ever been privileged to undergo this amazing experience called life! Add to that the reality that you had to fight off 400 trillion other sperm just to exist! Surely this realisation would make you understand that there is a purpose to your existence; you were not born to simply work hard and pay bills!

Prayers

- ◊ *"God help me to sharpen my skills like an axe so that I do not exert more strength than is necessary, grant me the wisdom that brings success in my endeavours."* (Ecclesiastes 10:10)

- ◊ *"I shall remember the Lord my God, for it is He who gives me power to get wealth, that He may establish His covenant with me which He swore to my fathers as it is this day. Therefore God, teach my hands to make wealth."* (Deuteronomy 8:17-18)

Ihu's Proclamations

- ◊ *"I am skilful and excellent in my work, therefore I will stand in honour before kings, I will not stand before obscure men."* (Proverbs 22-29)

- ◊ *"I have diligent hands that makes rich."* (Proverbs: 10-4)

Ihu's Reflections

- ◊ What area do you need to develop more skills in?

- ◊ Consider the brain as a muscle which needs to be exercised every day! What steps will you take daily to develop your skills?

- ◊ Remember, the acquisition of skills takes diligence, patience and, of course, perseverance.

Chapter Five
Gifts in Three Parts

"I'm about to do good works which I have prepared for you in advance to do"
(Ephesians 2:10)

The populist view is that human beings consist of mind and body; more recently, this has evolved to mind, body and spirit. However, I will extend this notion to say that we humans have a tripartite nature and exist in the three planes of the spirit, body and soul, which is made up of the mind, will and emotions.

1. The Mind: A Citadel of Intellect

Often considered the epicentre of human intelligence, the mind is a remarkable amalgamation of neural networks, synapses, and cognitive processes. From problem-solving to creative endeavours, the mind is our cognitive powerhouse, shaping our perceptions and understanding of the world. (*Cognitive Science Journal, Journal of Neurology Research Reviews*)

2. The Body: A Marvel of Biological Engineering

With its intricate systems and organs, the physical form is a testament to the brilliance of biological engineering. From the cardiovascular system ensuring oxygen supply, to the musculoskeletal system facilitating movement, the body is a complex organism finely tuned for survival and adaptation. (Rao et al, *Textbook of Medical Physiology and Human Anatomy*)

3. The Soul: The Enigma Beyond

The third facet introduces the enigmatic concept of the soul or consciousness. Beyond the mechanistic interplay of neurons, consciousness gives rise to self-awareness and subjective experiences, even spiritual ones. Exploring the nature of consciousness leads us into the realms of philosophy, psychology, and even quantum physics and theology. (Dennett, *Consciousness Explained*)

Your conscious mind controls the way you think, and your subconscious mind controls the way you feel. All our decisions are made based on how we think rather than how we feel. However, our outcomes are, to a large extent, dependent on how we feel.

INNER WORLD

Emotional	Spiritual
Mental	Physical

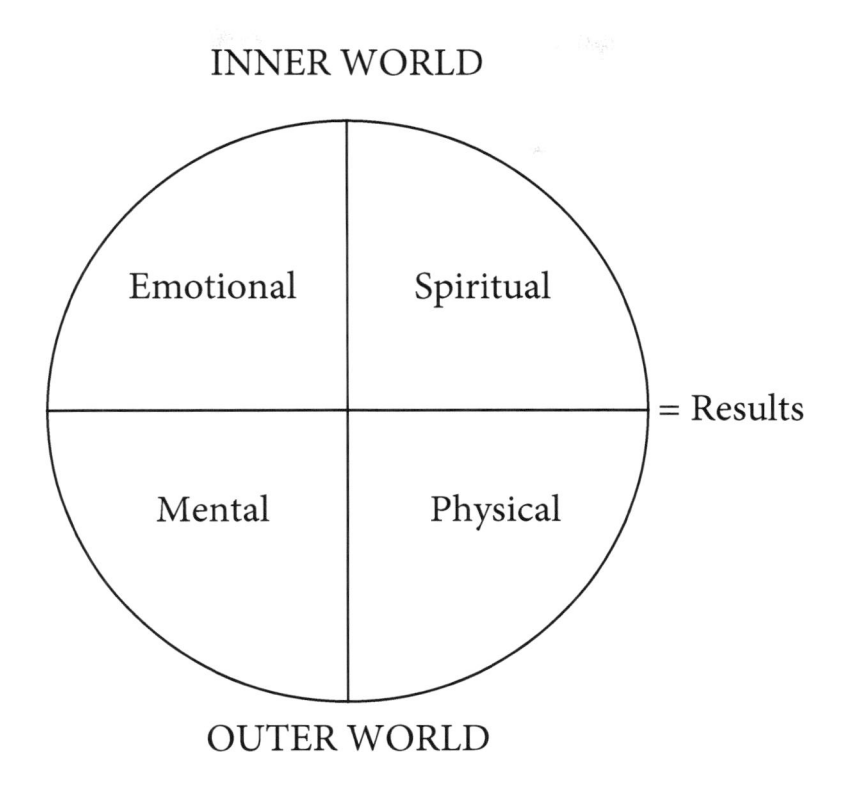

= Results

OUTER WORLD

A gift is a propensity for something, the seeds of which are usually seen when one is a child. Mastery in that gift is developed with practice, such as driving. The winning combination is to develop your natural gifts through constant practice to master them, and therefore becoming skilled in them. There is nothing wrong with functioning in all three levels of existence – spirit, soul and body, according to what the situation requires. These are the things that make us unique as human beings and makes us stand out from each other as individuals.

As we are tripartite beings, so also are our gifts given based on the three dimensions of our being.

1. **Your spiritual gifts** release illuminate or sets you and others free from unseen and intangible challenges exhorting the kingdom of God.

2. **Your soul gifts** (your mind, will and emotion) are to help bring comfort and relief to a distinct group of people soothing a pain in the soul. This usually comes from your painful experiences which leaves an indelible mark on your soul. However, it also qualifies you to help others going through the same situation, because we are not qualified to help someone through a challenging situation, unless we have been through it ourselves.

3. **Your physical gifts** are the gifts that are seen and represent things that can be produced, such as a book, clothing, cakes, carpentry, or even a service that brings financial gain in the physical realm. Your physical gifts solve a problem for humanity, bring you joy and bring joy to the world. It also honours God your master when used.

My soul gift is healing, my physical gift is creativity in fashion design and styling, and my spiritual gift is prophecy.

All our gifts (spiritual, soul and physical) honour God when used. When this happens, we are acting as God's true heirs, fulfilling His will for humanity on Earth and bringing forth the manifestation of His kingdom on Earth. Thy Kingdom come as it were.

Do you see the face of a proud father or mother when their little girl is decked out in all her Christmas finery, bow and all? It may not be for any specific reason but for the pleasure of the parent to observe the beauty of his or her child. It is a father or mother's pride and joy. How do you think a parent who bought you a beautiful dress and shoes would feel when they want to show you off to their friends? You come down in your raggedy clothes rather than the beautiful clothes they bought you? You make them feel shame and disappointment, that's what!

So also does God take pride when you show off your talents. God wants to show you off to the world through the showcasing of your gifts and talents which are an expression of who He is, and this is for His glory! He wants to beam with pride when you display your talents, be it that soothing tenor voice, that piano recital, that beautiful dress you made, your academic prowess, or superb engineering ability. Do not hide your talents, show them off!

> *"You are the light of the world.*
> *A town built on a hill cannot be hidden."*
>
> (Matthew 5:14-16)

When you are a light on a hill displaying your talents to the world, you light up other people's worlds by ministering to them in some way; you are showing them a piece or representation of God's personality and being, bringing a beam of joy and hope in the process.

- ◊ You may also **ignite** a passion within them.
- ◊ You **encourage** them and show them what is possible.
- ◊ You **minister** to them, perhaps to a downcast soul by uplifting their spirits.

Navigating through multiple giftings

To make it even more interesting, on each plane of existence, a person may be endowed with more than one gift. For instance, with the gift of spirituality, some people may operate in the five-fold ministry of teaching, prophecy, evangelism, healing and the apostolic. When it comes to physical skills, they may be gifted in administration, DIY, leadership and organisational skills. In terms of natural gifts, one individual may be gifted at sports, the spoken and written word, or have creative skills in art or music.

The brain is a complex organ that processes information, controls body functions, and houses thoughts and emotions, enabling individuals to master several skills at once.

The brain is segmented into regions called lobes which isolate its functions to specific areas.

- ◊ The frontal lobe (front of the brain) controls your body movement, personality, problem-solving, concentration, planning, emotional reactions, sense of smell, the meaning of words, and general speech.

- ◊ Your parietal lobe (upper middle of the brain) controls your sense of touch and pressure, sense of taste, and bodily awareness.

- ◊ The limbic lobe (middle of the brain) controls emotions.

- ◊ The temporal lobe (middle of the brain) governs your sense of hearing, ability to recognise others, emotions, and long-term memory.

◊ The occipital lobe (back of the brain) controls the important sense of sight.

◊ The cerebellum (lower back of the brain) governs fine motor control, balance and coordination.

Left vs. Right Brain: What's the difference?

The left and right hemispheres of the brain are responsible for different functions. The left hemisphere is often associated with logical thinking, language and analytical skills, whilst the right hemisphere is linked to creativity, intuition and spatial awareness. However, both hemispheres work together for most cognitive tasks, and stronger skills result from the two hemispheres working well together, so the idea of strict left or right brain dominance is oversimplified.

Human beings are so interesting and complex that we cannot be boxed in and classified as being one thing or the other. My second son can be considered to function on both the right and left brain. He functions in the creative in making up jokes, writing screenplays, and in drama. He is also a proficient pianist. On the other hand, he has always shown ability in logic, reasoning and mathematics, even as a 10-year-old child and now at the age of 16, he still excels in these areas. In fact, he wants to combine a profession in acting with a profession as a physician, and we are not limiting him or forcing him to take one direction but to pursue the extent of all his God-given potentials.

Similarly, my eldest son has always shown proficiency and natural ability as a sportsman. However, he also has a very retentive memory and debates well.

Just as in the parable of the five talents where some servants were either given one, three or five gifts, so are some people blessed with more than one talent. Every unique plant or flower needs to be cultivated by a skilled horticulturist, so does the multi-talented person have to cultivate their gifts or the parents of such a child enable them to develop these talents.

A great example of someone that displayed a variety of gifts in all three levels was Jesus of Nazareth. The Bible is usually very particular about noting down the profession of personalities, and Jesus was a carpenter. Before his ministry started, he was skilled and made his living in carpentry. As his ministry grew, the spiritual gifts which he displayed as a child became more evident, such as in performing the first miracle of turning water into wine at the wedding in Cana. In terms of spiritual gifts, Jesus was indeed the master because he performed many documented healing miracles.

He was also a great teacher, as he was lovingly known as Raboni by his disciples and followers, which means Teacher in Hebrew. Indeed, Jesus used parables to make the many concepts about the kingdom of God easier to understand for the masses. Jesus prophesied extensively, turning many into Christians by evangelising and encouraging his disciples whom he was training to do the same. The Apostolic was seen in him as he built the church of God through His disciples. Jesus also demonstrated exceptional wisdom (a spiritual gift) in all he did; such as the way he answered questions, challenges from Roman soldiers, and even on the temptation on the mount, where he was challenged and withstood Satan for 40 days and nights. Jesus' ministry demonstrated the tripartite function exceptionally well, as he used natural giftings in leadership to lead his disciples and other followers.

Grasping that we are complex beings and we do not exist on one plane will help us to understand how to place and navigate our different giftings.

Prayers

◊ *"God thank you for giving me differing gifts according to the grace that is given to me, help me to use them to your glory and in helping your people: let me prophesy in proportion to my faith; let me use it in ministering in teaching and in exhortation. Help me to give, with liberality; lead with diligence and show mercy, with cheerfulness."* (Romans 12:6-8)

Ihu's Proclamations

◊ *"God will bless the works of my hands."* (Deuteronomy 28:12)

◊ *"I am wealthy – God shall teach my hands to make wealth."* (Deuteronomy 8:18)

◊ I am a great fashion designer/singer/actor/artist (you fill in the blank!).

◊ I use all my gifts to my benefit and to the benefit of those around me.

Ihu's Reflections

- ◊ We have a tripartite nature, existing in three planes: the spirit, the body and the soul, which in turn is made up of the mind, will and emotions.

- ◊ Take a moment to consider what your spirit, soul and body gifts are.

- ◊ Have you been using these gifts?

- ◊ Consider how you can better use them to serve yourself, your community and to bring Glory to God.

Chapter Six
Mountains and Mantles

*"And here is the mind which hath wisdom.
The seven heads are seven mountains."*

(Revelation 17:9)

You have dominion of a domain – a mountain is a domain and faith unlocks it.

Many people lose hope and give up easily due to a lack of understanding of who they really are, what they are made for, and who they have been called to serve. Even the Bible says that we should not cast our pearls before swine, meaning that what we offer to the world is not for everyone and the sooner we identify this, the more energy we conserve in serving the people we are called to serve.

It all starts with an understanding of who you are and what your identity is. Once you understand this, all your choices will fall into place and life will start making more sense. You will avoid a lot of wasted time, disappointment, and a life of mediocrity.

You will dominate in your own domain but what is your domain? Just as each one of us has a unique thumbprint and set of talents, we also have a unique domain, an area or ideal environment for those skill sets to thrive. Our life's mission should be not only to discover our unique talents, but also the domain where they are assigned to. If the skills and talents we have are gifts, then the domain we are assigned to is the soil.

I believe that an exploration of the combination of both elements will bring about a perfect synergy for success in your life's purpose.

The best description of different areas where one's gifts can function that I have seen is the Seven Mountains of Influence.

The Seven Mountains of Influence are the spheres of influence that shape the values that form society. The movement of the Seven Mountains of Influence (sometimes known as the Seven Mountains of Culture) started in 1975 as evangelicals Loren Cunningham, Bill Bright and Francis Schaeffer purported to have received a message from God to invade the "seven spheres" of society, identified as family, religion, education, media, arts and entertainment, business, and government.

- ◊ Family: The sphere of relationships and identity.
- ◊ Religion: The sphere of faith and spirituality.
- ◊ Education: The sphere of learning and knowledge.
- ◊ Media: The sphere of communication and information.

- ◊ Arts and Entertainment: The sphere of creativity and expression.
- ◊ Business: The sphere of economy and stewardship.
- ◊ Government: The sphere of authority and justice.

I believe there is an 8th mountain which was not considered initially, and that is the Mountain of Health and Healing.

I also think that the mountains broadly align with the five-fold ministry framework as I illustrate below.

Mountain	Five-Fold Ministry	Archetype
Family	Pastoral	Esther
Religion	Prophetic	Elijah
Education	Teaching	Jesus
Media	Evangelism	Paul
Arts and Entertainment	Worship	David
Business	Administration	Joseph
Government	Apostolic	Daniel
Healthcare	Healing	Jesus

The idea of the Seven Mountains of Influence did not fully come to fruition until a meeting between Cunningham and

Lance Wallnau in 2000. The movement came to prominence following the publication of Wallnau and Bill Johnson's book, *Invading Babylon: The 7 Mountain Mandate*.

> *"Now it shall come to pass in the latter days that the mountain of the Lord's house shall be established on the top of the mountains."*
>
> (Isaiah 2:2)

This scripture speaks of our mandate as humans to have dominion in all the areas of influence.

How can we achieve dominion?

> *"A city that is set on a hill cannot be hidden. Nor do they light a lamp and put it under a basket, but on a lampstand, and it gives light to all who are in the house. Let your light so shine before men, that they may see your good works and glorify your father in heaven."*
>
> (Matthew 5:14-16)

Indeed, we are called to be the light of the world and to stand on top of our respective mountains, dominating and influencing others. However, you must first catch that fire of passion before you can illuminate others. When you are not lit, you cannot illuminate the darkness of others. Light up your fire first, seek that unique area that you can operate in with total sovereignty, and master that area. Only then will you have the full ability to inspire others and the authority to influence them to follow in your footsteps.

I believe I am called to function in the Mountain of family and my social enterprise Cedarcube's mandate is to Heal,

Empower, Bond and Connect, with a mission to heal hearts and strengthen families. I am passionate about this area, and I seem to have a natural affinity towards it. I believe that most of society's ills, such as abuse, mental health problems and criminal delinquencies, would be eradicated if addressed at the root level of the family.

I find that a person doesn't normally choose a Mountain to function in; they are called to it, almost like an unseen mantle they wear. It is a natural fit to your disposition, like a well-measured and tailored glove. Your personality and uniqueness will give an indication of the Mountain you are called to and would best function in.

As naturally as I fit into the Mountain of Family, my husband is called to the Governmental Mountain. His personality and make-up supports this calling; he has a natural aura of authority and leadership about him, some would say a 'presence'. He is now a District Councillor in my local area of Essex but prior to this, he would be called to speak at events and would be given leadership roles in most organisations he joined, both paid and unpaid. Indeed, he is also a Non-Executive Director of several charity boards as well as sitting as an executive in the Local Government Authority (LGA).

Those who understand energy and have discernment will perceive the mantle that people carry. Many would often prophesy that my husband, Chidi, would be in government. This happened when we were courting. We were attending our church and in the middle of the service, the pastor pointed to him and said, "You will be a key person in government in Nigeria!"

Now, he is functioning in government in the UK. Mantles move with you no matter your geographical location, and Chidi has also recently been made Vice-Chair of the Nigerian Councillors in the UK so watch out, that initial prophecy may still be fully realised one way or another!

The people that you get to 'sit under', such as mentors and those in your circle, as well as the general circumstances of life that shape you, are all an indication of the mantle that you carry. My father was a politician before he passed away – what is the likelihood that my husband (now a politician) would end up marrying a politician's daughter?! The similarities do not end there. Chidi and I bought the house that I grew up in and this is the same vicinity where my husband was made a District Councillor. It is as if that mantle of leadership passed from my father to my husband or in some strange way, subconscious forces were working in my husband's life to lead him on the path he should go. I believe this is the same force working in all our lives if we pause to reflect on it.

I am named after my grandmother by the very traditional Igbo name of Ihuaku, which means 'the face of wealth' or 'one who has a wealthy fortune or future'. This did not only stem from my father's reverence for his mother, a renowned and successful businesswoman in her day, but also because the year I was born was my father's most successful in business to date.

I have always shown a good understanding and leaning towards entrepreneurship and business. I once got in trouble in school because I took some free pens and other stationery that my father got from work when he was working as a sales rep for a pharmaceutical company, to sell in school. I would often walk to and from school and skip lunch to save my transport and dinner money, such was my determination! I started making money at the age of 13 when I was doing paper rounds with my brother before school. I also befriended a mother with three children in our council estate when I was 15 and she trusted me so much that she would pay me to babysit her children.

My talents for fashion and ability to seek out ways to make money was a clear indication of the mantle of business and stewardship that I walk in. Even now, I have multiple businesses and regularly have to make a conscious effort to stem the flow of business ideas I get so that I can focus on the ones I have on hand. The multi-coloured mantle of Joseph is clearly very strong in my life.

It seems that I am passing on this mantle to my youngest son who showed signs of being a keen entrepreneur from about the age of five. He would market, negotiate and charge his way through services or products that most children would give for free, such as marbles or snacks. For as long as I can remember, he would nag me to take him to sell stuff at car boot sales to make some money. He has the same gritty determination that most entrepreneurs seem to be born with; he never gives up on anything he wants and is very disciplined.

When he was 10 years old, he wanted an Oculus video game which cost a couple of hundred pounds. I told him that the only way I would consider getting this for him would be if he paid for half of it. He set to work, inventing different ways of raising funds, from washing our cars to cleaning skirting boards to mowing the lawn. He managed to successfully raise £120 in no time at all! Needless to say, he is the one in the house who always has cash readily available to lend and when he does, he doesn't fail to add interest should anyone fail to pay back on time!

My oldest son seems to also have that same mantle of leadership that my husband has; he has a great retentive memory for facts and dates, and a charismatic aura that attracts leadership to him. He is now studying the traditional subjects of English Literature, history and psychology, the art of understanding how the human mind works. He is very fair in his dealings and empathetic to people's plights. As previously mentioned, he has a natural talent for sports, but these may all be part of the appeal. Indeed, Lady Tanni Grey-Thompson who now sits in the House of Lords, and Pelé, the prolific Brazilian footballer, were successful sports people in their respective countries – the UK and Brazil – who became loved and respected activists and politicians in their own rights.

Simply because you have a talent in one area does not mean you cannot be called to a different Mountain. As previously mentioned, my second son is showing great talent in music and the performing arts, but also has a phenomenal brain for the sciences and wants to be a doctor. Indeed, you can be called to influence more than one Mountain throughout your lifetime.

Have you paid the price for your mantle?

I find that in most cases, having access or the keys to gain dominion in any sphere or Mountain does not come cheap. It usually takes some form of struggle or sacrifice. Taking an example from the lives of some of the biblical archetypes discussed, we can see this played out.

> **Joseph:** Experienced betrayal from his brothers and experienced incarceration and being lied against. However, in the end, he gained the key to authority in government.

Ruth: Experienced severe loss and separation from all she knew when her sons and husband died, but in return, she gained a legacy and inheritance of the kingdom of Israel through David and eventually God's kingdom by being one of the ancestors of Jesus Christ.

Esther: Was an orphan girl who was willing to sacrifice her life, going to the extreme of fasting for three days to save her people from certain death.

"Go, gather all the Jews who are present in Shushan, and fast for me; neither eat nor drink for three days, night or day. My maids and I will fast likewise. And so I will go to the king, which is against the law; and if I perish, I perish!"

(Esther 4:16)

Her gamble and sacrifice paid off and she gained favour with the King and more authority in the kingdom. Mordecai received the King's seal and signet ring which had belonged to Haman and he was allowed to make decrees on behalf of the King which would have been heavily influenced by Esther. One of those decrees allowed the Jews to defend themselves against anyone who would want to attack them under the decree influenced by Haman.

Job: Endured extreme suffering and loss from all he owned including his children, his businesses and his cattle. He also became very sick and eventually lost his wife. However, when he was restored, his fortunes reversed, and he had even more than he had before.

Prayers

- ◊ *"God, help me to identify the mountain and mantle you have called me to and help me walk in authority and influence in it."*

Ihu's Proclamations:

- ◊ *"I have dominion over the works of my hands; all things are under my feet."* (Psalm 8:6)
- ◊ *"I shall have dominion also from sea to sea, and from the River to the ends of the earth."* (Psalm 72:8)
- ◊ *"I have the authority to trample on serpents and scorpions and over all the power of the enemy and nothing shall by any means hurt me."* (Luke 10:19)

Ihu's Reflections

- ◊ Looking over your life and all the experiences you have gone through, which Mountain do you think you have been called to?
- ◊ Take a moment to reflect upon your life: which mantle do you think is upon you?

Chapter Seven
Keys and Access

"The key of the house of David I will lay on his shoulder; So he shall open, and no one shall shut; And he shall shut, and no one shall open"

(Isaiah 22:22)

There are a certain set of people who are gatekeepers to a mountain and domain. They are the key and the one that opens the door to the domain. They are well connected and stand out as yielding influence in that specific area.

To wield influence in a particular domain, one must usually go through a challenging and difficult experience in that area. In my experience and observation, there are a special set of people that go through exceptionally difficult and painful early life experiences, which then equip them for the journey ahead. Through their tough experiences, they develop strength and resilience, and through difficulty, they learn how to solve the life problems they face. Through suffering, they develop compassion, empathy and a desire to ease the suffering of others. These beacons of light become guiding lights to others in the Mountain they have been called to influence. Often shaped by adversity in childhood or adolescence, they are marked by a wisdom beyond their years. In the case of legends such as Alexander the Great and Michael Jackson (the King of Pop), though they died quite young, the phenomenal legacy they left continues to live on and impact generations way after their time. Once they have gone through their trials, they are qualified and anointed – chosen, if you will – for their mission and life purpose. They are then given the keys to the gates of their Mountain.

One of such people is the great Robert Nesta Marley, who died from cancer at 36 years old. Bob was born in Jamaica to a white father and a Jamaican mother in February 1945. His father abandoned him, and at six years old, he was sent to live with a distant family friend whilst his mother relocated to Delaware. He grew up on the tough streets of Trench Town in West Kingston, which at the time was likened to an open sewer! His adopted parents gave him a guitar and he formed his band, The Wailers, which included Peter Tosh and Bunny Wailer. Soon after, he took up Rastafarianism which is a religion linked to Christianity. It is influenced by the philosophies in popular quasi-biblical prophecy of the Ethiopian Emperor Haile Selassie, as the Lion of Judah and African redeemer.

Bob's music united political factions in Jamaica and still continues to unite people today. His music and legacy continues; his album *Legend*, a posthumous collection of his works, became the bestselling reggae album ever with international sales reaching more than 12 million copies. He carries on being the 11th highest earning artist even in death. Bob used his influence of the entertainment Mountain to make bold political and humanitarian statements which touched his country and the rest of the world, and continues to do so to date.

Bob's story is not unique; this pattern repeats itself. I recently met a lady who was abandoned by her parents after a divorce. Her mother was forced to abandon her and flee to another country because her father was about to kill her along with her new lover in a jealous rage. She ended up living with her father for a while; however, he also neglected her when he found new love, leaving her to fend for herself at the tender age of 11 years old. She became a delinquent and three years later, she left school. Somehow, she ended up raising enough money to buy an ice cream van, earning £400 a day.

At the age of 18, she happened to come across a woman who owned a modelling agency and wanted to sell it as she had fallen on hard times. Brazenly, she said she would buy it and that started off her upward journey into enterprise. She is now a millionaire in her own right, helping others doing good in the world achieve their best. Her early life trials were instrumental in giving her the skill set to be a source of influence in the business world.

Access can be granted through a number of keys. The keys give the access, and access in turn grants favour, authority and dominion.

Universal keys to access

🗝 Words

> "Death and life are in the power of the tongue,
> And those who love it will eat its fruit."
>
> (Proverbs 18:21)

Your words penetrate the air and give you access to create what you have pronounced. God, or a universal source, created the world with the power of words; therefore, it is no wonder that our words are a creative force, because we have that same power. This is the origin of affirmations. Indeed, what you believe and affirm becomes your reality, whether positive or negative. Knowing that we have the power to create our own reality, why not focus on the positive?

🗝 Sowing

> "While the earth remains, seedtime and harvest, cold and heat, winter and summer, and day and night shall not cease."
>
> (Genesis 8:22)

This is an age-old farming principle that your seed breaks the ground and gives you access to reap a harvest. Similarly, giving – whether it be of money or investment – also gives you access. What you sow you shall reap.

> "Do not be deceived, God is not mocked; for whatever a man sows, that he will also reap. For he who sows to his flesh will of the flesh reap corruption, but he who sows to the Spirit will of the Spirit reap everlasting life."
>
> (Galatians 6:7)

Knowing this universal principle, why not sow good seeds? Your investment will give you access and come back to you multiplied in a fruitful harvest. What do you have to give? Your time, your money, your talents? All give you access – givers never lack anything.

🗝 Gratitude

> *"Enter His gates with thanksgiving,*
> *And into His courts with praise."*
> (Psalm 100:4)

Gratitude is a universal key to opening doors of abundance. When you are grateful for something, you are telling the universal intelligence and divine source of all things that you appreciate it, and you want more of the same.

Conversely, a lack of gratitude translates to a rejection of a gift. This sends a message that you don't want more of the same from where the gift came from.

Some people are blessed but they do not know it, which is why they continue to see lack in their lives. Gratitude is a way of acknowledging the blessings in your life and in so doing, you agree with it and agreement brings multiplication. Acknowledgement is agreement and agreement equates to alignment.

The power of gratitude for both the giver and the receiver can be illustrated in Luke 17:11-19 in the Parable of the 10 Lepers:

"And one of them, when he saw that he was healed, returned, and with a loud voice glorified God, and fell down on his face

at His feet, giving Him thanks. And he was a Samaritan. So Jesus answered and said, 'Were there not ten cleansed? But where are the nine? Were there not any found who returned to give glory to God except this foreigner?' And He said to him, 'Arise, go your way. Your faith has made you well.'"

Jesus was pleased with the leper who came back to give thanks. As a result, Jesus pronounced that his gratitude had made him well which was an unusual statement because he had already been healed along with the other nine lepers. Perhaps Jesus was pointing to a further intangible and internal wellness beyond the initial surface cleansing?

🗝 Knowledge

"Wisdom is the principal thing; Therefore, get wisdom. And in all your getting, get understanding. Exalt her, and she will promote you; she will bring you honour, when you embrace her. She will place on your head an ornament of grace; A crown of glory she will deliver to you."

(Proverbs 4:7-9)

Wisdom is the application of knowledge and knowledge gives you access. Knowledge is power. Knowledge and understanding of a principle can grant you power; people will pay dearly for this knowledge, giving you the cutting edge and making you the go-to person in your industry which automatically translates to wealth. It was no surprise that when Solomon was asked by God what he wanted, he did not ask for riches or power, but for wisdom. When he was granted this, he received wealth, honour and riches too.

🗝️ Gifts and Talents

> *"A Man's gift makes room for him and brings him before great men."*
> (Proverbs 18:16)

Your gifts and talents gives you access and brings you before great people. In every kingdom, it is always the greatest artisans that are called upon to build palaces and temples, and indeed to dress kings and queens. Royalty always demands the best in the land and if you have honed your craft to the level of excellence, then guess what? You will also be called upon to serve royalty.

Take, for instance, Sir Christopher Wren, born in England in 1632. He was a notable brilliant architect as well as mathematician, astronomer and physicist. He was called upon to build 52 churches in London following the Great Fire of London in 1666, including St Paul's Cathedral which is regarded as his masterpiece. His works are now some of the most famous of London's landmarks, recognised across the world for their grand designs and palatial stateliness, including some of Hampton Court Palace and the Old Royal Naval College in Greenwich. Wren was knighted for his services on 14th November 1673.

Indeed, all over the world we also see other great masters of their crafts, such as Michelangelo who painted the Sistine Chapel in the Roman Vatican city between 1508 and 1512 for many to marvel at for years to come.

There are also spiritual gifts which are themselves intangible; however, they give a tangible outcome which gives access.

Billy Graham

On 14th July 1950, Billy Graham was invited to the White House to meet President Harry Truman. The visit was arranged by two congressmen: Joe Bryson of South Carolina, and Herbert C. Bonner of North Carolina.

Thousands came to the saving knowledge of Jesus Christ when the late Queen Elizabeth II invited him to the chapel of Windsor Castle and then onwards to hold crusades in Glasgow, Scotland, and London's Wembley Stadium. This friendship spanned six decades and in 1983, another US president, Ronald Reagan, invited Graham for a dinner at the White House held in honour of Queen Elizabeth's visit. Billy Graham's spiritual gifts though intangible brought tangible transformations and benefits. As a result of them, he enjoyed personal access to leaders, great men and women and indeed royalty.

Grace, mercy and favour are other free spiritual gifts which are intangible but are granted to individuals as a way of equipping them for their area of impact. These are not granted freely but often through some process of life struggle, and they are given for a purpose.

🗝 Service

> *"I beseech you therefore, brethren, by the mercies of God, that you present your bodies a living sacrifice, holy, acceptable to God, which is your reasonable service."*
>
> (Romans 12:1)

Service grants access to promotion. We can see this in the lives of servicemen and women, who have sacrificed their lives to serve their countries, being given great honours for their bravery. Indeed, those who sacrifice their lives and times in service to underprivileged parts of society often gain awards of the highest order, such as the OBE, MBE, CBE, a Knighthood or a Damehood in the United Kingdom, or the presidential awards in the USA.

The best way to learn has always been to serve and it is no surprise that great leaders are often great servants.

The late Queen Elizabeth II served her country tirelessly for seven decades and will be fondly remembered and missed for her service, not only to her country, but to the commonwealth and the world.

Jesus Christ himself exemplified servant leadership, particular in the image of him washing the feet of his disciples.

We spoke previously about the tradition of apprenticeships all over the world and following a period of service, it is universally agreed that the apprentice has gained sufficient skill and knowledge in their craft to earn the title of serviceman and, eventually, master. No one can deny the access earnt through the visible sacrifice of service.

Sacrifice

"God presented Christ as a sacrifice of atonement, through the shedding of his blood – to be received by faith."
(Romans 3:25)

Sacrifice has been an age-old principle to obtain a thing that is greatly desired. Sacrifice is a form of exchange and when we sacrifice something dear to us, we are sending a signal to the universe that we are willing to pay a high price to obtain that object we desire. Many cultures across the world and throughout history have used sacrifice, from animals to the extreme case of human sacrifice, to obtain something they perceive that is of greater good, whether it is to bring an end to a famine or to assure victory in war.

Indeed, rather perversely, war and the sacrifice of a few for a certain time can be seen as a sacrifice to obtain longer lasting peace for the masses.

God made the ultimate sacrifice by sending his son Jesus in embodied form to die for our sins. The Bible states that when he died, he rose on the third day having gone to Hell or Hades to obtain the keys of life and death.

"I am He who lives, and was dead, and behold, I am alive forevermore. Amen. And I have the keys of Hades and of Death." (Revelations 1:18)

Many religions today still combine the sacrifice of food or pleasures through fasting as a way of consecrating their bodies as living sacrifices and to gain greater purity and spiritual ascendance. This is to gain intimacy with God and obtain answers to prayers and supplications, or to gain greater spiritual understanding and revelation.

🗝️ Obedience

> *"Behold, to obey is better than sacrifice.*
> *And to heed than the fat of rams."*
>
> (1 Samuel 15-22)

Obedience gives you access and alignment to divine universal timing and opportunities. I have many moments in my life to illustrate the importance of listening to your inner voice and obeying its leading.

Towards the end of 2019, I was looking for a new job. I had attended several interviews, both for permanent and part-time temporary work. I had an offer of a permanent role as a Commercial Manager in the London Borough of Waltham Forest. Everything looked great on paper; it was near home, the pay was decent, it was stable and had good benefits. However, something about the role did not align with me.

After one month, I subsequently received another job offer, but it was a temporary role with the Ministry of Justice, with no benefits or job stability. However, the pay amounted to double the annual pay for the other role and the contract was for six months.

I decided to take the risk and hand in my notice for the permanent role and took up the temporary role with the Ministry of Justice. I started my new role in January 2020 having only completed three months with the London Borough of Waltham Forest. However, I did not regret my decision. I was able to save up enough money within two years to purchase our home, something that had eluded us for four years.

Recently, I had a nagging direction to apply to be a UN delegate. I had come across the form online for some months, but I had put it on the back burner. The nagging voice urging me to apply would not go away until I finally completed the application. Within two weeks, I received the response that I had been selected as one of the UK delegates to the United Nations for the Promotion of Human Rights for Women and Girls!

I have found that whenever you have a strong urge to take a certain action, you must listen to that inner voice because it is universal intelligence trying to align you with your higher self for the greater good. Many people are not where they are supposed to be today, but instead are living a life of compromise because they failed to act on a lead from their inner voice and guidance.

Friendliness

"A man who has friends must himself be friendly."
(Proverbs 18:24)

Your smile and having a friendly disposition is a key which grants you access to the hearts of men and women. There is a saying that "your network is your net worth" and that we inhabit this earth with other humans who are the harbingers of both good and bad. Therefore, it is to your advantage to win the hearts and minds of other humans by being pleasant and friendly.

I received my first ever opportunity to showcase at African Fashion Week London following a meeting with a lady I was friendly with at church. She told me about five part-sponsored places by *New African Woman* magazine for new designers to participate in African Fashion Week. I had to make a quick decision and commit, even though I did not have a readily available collection. That was big faith in action! The point is that the lady would not have considered presenting me with that opportunity if I had not been friendly with her. Your friendliness yields great results!

🗝 Intimacy

> *"Call to me and I will answer you and will tell you great and hidden things that you have not known."*
>
> (Jeremiah 33:3)

Intimacy relates to friendliness but involves a deep knowing and the admittance into privileged knowledge and information not available to everyone. At this level of intimacy, nothing is hidden. Indeed, there are few people who are privileged to enjoy this level of intimacy with God, the infinite source of all things.

"Surely the Lord God does nothing unless He reveals His secret to His servants the prophets." (Amos 3:7)

This privilege, though accessible to all, is only available to those who have paid the price to obtain it.

In the Bible, we see the benefits of intimacy played out again and again.

Esther received favour from the king because of her intimacy with him, and through that intimacy, managed to save the Israelites from ethnic cleansing.

Potiphar entrusted Joseph with everything in his house due to his competence in managing his resources. Subsequently he became second only to Pharaoh because of his trustworthiness and leadership abilities. Joseph's honesty and competence made him an asset to his masters and caused them to trust him with their secrets and treasures granting him intimacy with them

Elisha through his intimacy with Elijah was able to receive a double portion of Elijah's prophetic anointing and symbolically Elijah's mantle.

🔑 Humility

> *"Humble yourselves before the Lord, and he will lift you up."*
>
> (James 4:10)

Humility gives you access to honour. It is indeed true that humility is a forerunner to elevation, whereas pride blocks access and leads to downfall.

"A man's pride will bring him low, But the humble in spirit will retain honour." (Proverbs 29:23)

People are less likely to come to the aid of someone who puts up the façade of not needing help or guidance. A person that has a pleasant and lowly demeanour is likely to attract more assistance, but this should not be mistaken for lack of confidence. It is possible to be confident but humble.

Prayers

- ◊ Oh God, open my eyes to see the keys you have given me and grant me the wisdom to use them effectively for your glory and the good of all.

- ◊ Oh God, help me to develop keys in _____ [name the areas that you are lacking in] so that I may walk more fully in my purpose

Ihu's Proclamations

- ◊ *"I have the keys of the kingdom of Heaven, and whatever I bind on earth shall be bound in Heaven, and whatever I loose on earth shall be loosed in Heaven."* (Matthew 16:19)

- ◊ *"I have on my shoulder the key of the house of David. I shall open, and none shall shut; and I shall shut, and none shall open."* (Isaiah 22:22)

Ihu's Reflections

- ◊ Have you recognised any of these keys and how they have been beneficial in your life?

- ◊ Now you know their power, how do you intend to use them more to benefit you and those around you in the attainment of your life purpose?

- ◊ Which keys do you need to work more on to develop?

Part Two

Resourcing Your Purpose

Chapter Eight
Assign Your Time, Appoint Your Life

*"To everything there is a season,
and a time to every purpose under the heaven."*

(Ecclesiastes 3:1)

Every dream, every promise, every opportunity you have been given, has a window and time assigned to it. Disobedience, using our own wisdom and procrastination will lead to missing these opportunities to detrimental effect. Many people are experiencing a lot of sorrow and pain today compounded with the reality of missed opportunities for this very reason. Therefore, do not be limited by your own wisdom, because the fear of God is the beginning of all wisdom; when God says move, drop everything else and move so that you can reap the rewards of obedience and God's promises for your life.

Time is the most quintessential and valuable resource that we have; more precious than money. Anything worth having in life takes time, labour, patience and perseverance

– creating a human, for instance, takes a good nine months of carrying a heavy load and then experiencing the pain to birth it into being. Does this mean it is not worth having? No! Quite the contrary.

Since time is so valuable, it is vital that we do not misuse it on activities that are underserving of its value.

"Do not cast your pearls before swine." (Matthew 7:6)

You need to send your time on 'assignment'. This means allocating what you will do with your time in advance. Don't only say what you will do, but also state when you will do it. In addition, with anything you are doing, ask yourself, *Why am I doing this and how does it fit into the bigger picture of my life plans and purpose?* When you start with assigning your time, you are on your way to living a purposeful life.

When you put a value on your time, you will realise how costly time misspent is. Anytime misused or mismatched with projects that don't contribute towards your life's bigger picture, equates to your time being misspent; you're literally pouring your life away.

However, it is vital that you do not fall into the trap of doing everything yourself. When you discover how precious your life is, then you will put value on the time you spend on various activities.

It is advisable to conduct an audit on how you spend your time. This is particularly important for mothers and wives who often spend a large proportion of their time nurturing others. Ask yourself, "Does it really matter who does the housework, as long as it is done?" Before you take on another chore, ask, "Am I the best person to do this? Would my time be better spent on something else right now?" If your children are off school on holiday, ask yourself if it would be better to spend time with them now or cleaning the house. If you cannot hire a cleaner, then consider whether it would be best to do it when everyone is asleep or even better doing it all together as a bonding exercise for the whole family, perhaps with some singing and dancing to elevate the activity even more!

It is worth thinking carefully about what you do and how you do it. The chart below will help in the decision-making process:

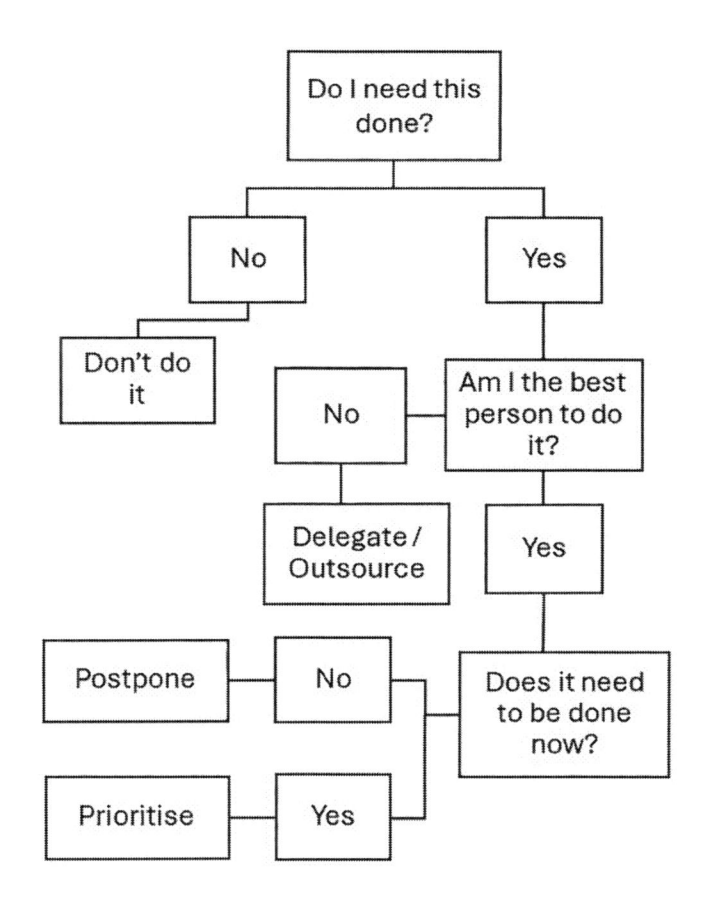

```
                    ┌──────────────┐
                    │ Do I need this│
                    │    done?     │
                    └──────┬───────┘
              ┌────────────┴────────────┐
            ┌─┴──┐                    ┌─┴──┐
            │ No │                    │Yes │
            └─┬──┘                    └─┬──┘
              │                         │
        ┌─────┴──┐                ┌─────┴─────┐
        │Don't do│      ┌────┐    │Am I the best│
        │   it   │      │ No ├────┤ person to do│
        └────────┘      └─┬──┘    │     it?    │
                          │       └─────┬─────┘
                    ┌─────┴────┐      ┌─┴──┐
                    │Delegate/ │      │Yes │
                    │Outsource │      └─┬──┘
                    └──────────┘        │
  ┌────────┐   ┌────┐            ┌──────┴──────┐
  │Postpone├───┤ No ├────────────┤Does it need │
  └────────┘   └────┘            │to be done   │
                                 │    now?     │
  ┌────────┐   ┌────┐            └─────────────┘
  │Prioritise├─┤Yes │
  └────────┘   └────┘
```

105

Procrastination, the time waster

Procrastination is putting things off to a tomorrow that never arrives. Procrastination can occur as a result of several issues, such as a lack of discipline or an inability to manage the time you have now. Procrastination often leads to wasted and missed opportunities because by the time you get round to doing those chores or writing that book, the deadline has been missed, the opportunity no longer exists or if it does, it is more costly to execute. Have you ever heard of the saying, *A stitch in time saves nine*? To give you an example, I ordered some goods from China, and I was hit with a FedEx bill. I kept forgetting to pay it. Each time I would receive an updated bill more expensive than the last as interest had been added on until I eventually paid it!

When you disobey or procrastinate with an instruction that God has given you for a certain time and season of your life, you will forever be playing catch up with your destiny because He is a God of new things. We operate in an ever moving and fluid universe and time does not stand still. Everything is in motion, so when you are finally ready to take action, things have most likely moved on!

Prayer against procrastination

- ◊ Oh God, grant me the grace to follow your instructions speedily in Jesus' name.
- ◊ Oh God, ensure that I do not miss my moment in Jesus' name.

Distraction, the time stealer

Distractions divert the soul's purpose. In the age of information, we are even more aware of what's going on in other people's lives (whether real or curated) through beautiful pictures and enhanced stories on social media and television.

This gives rise to envy. Envy is a dangerous, polluting energy which confuses your authentic energy. It makes you think you want something that's not really for you and you lose focus and start pursuing something different from what you have been called to.

Trying to replicate the lifestyle and success of others is a futile exercise because we do not have the same mission and purpose in life; the more time spent watching and attempting to live the life of others, the less time spent living your own. This can be damaging as it makes you feel that your humble efforts are insufficient. It leads to a pattern of trying to replicate a certain lifestyle and this can be detrimental to you living a life true to yourself, your specific journey and your purpose. Rather than directing you, it distracts you and makes you develop a fear of missing out and a scattered mentality, rather than the focused approach of a life truly directed by your soul's purpose.

Indeed, it is easier in this modern age to feel like you're not doing enough, pursuing the latest money-making trend – but to what end? If this activity causes you to take a longer route, then why not simply take the short cut and do that one thing you love doing? If the distractions ultimately divert you from your soul's purpose, why pay attention to them? Yet many get embroiled in activity that does not ultimately serve their purpose due to peer pressure and fear of missing out, letting their minds believe the false narrative that they must do what everyone else is doing.

The mind is like a babbling brook that always rises to the surface, yet the soul is heavy and still, like a rock; listen to it!

We may often lose track of our path and get derailed due to distractions, the 'shiny toy' syndrome, distracted by the newest get-rich-quick scheme or venture or the newest fad. We may even lose heart that the gains we anticipated are taking too long to realise. However, I implore you to stay focused – remember your reasons for starting on this journey, learn from your mistakes, get some rest and recover, pick yourself up, and get back on track!

I believe that distraction comes as a result of unassigned time, so if you assign your time, even your rest time, you will determine your life.

"Let me pass through your land; I will keep strictly to the road, and I will turn neither to the right nor to the left." (Deuteronomy 2:27)

Where there is a promise (of God), there is a propaganda (of the enemy), so keep pressing on with your promise and avoid the distractions and lies of Satan!

Prayer against distractions

- ◊ Oh God, deliver me from all distractions, detractors and diverters from my divine purpose in Jesus' name.

- ◊ Oh God, help me to discern destiny distractions in Jesus' name.

The need for patience

Patience is the incubator that manifests greatness. The greatest achievements in the world took time to develop and the greatest masterpieces, architectural wonders and works of art took time to create.

Patience is a virtue because when you're impatient, it makes you sabotage your goal by causing you to produce substandard work or worse still, give up on the process all together. Furthermore, it causes you to lack discernment, leaving you to be susceptible to falling prey to counterfeit solutions. The enemy comes in a hurry with a counterfeit, but the real deal takes time. Do not fall into a pit in a hurry; be patient and wait on the Lord.

Anything worth having in life takes time, work, patience and perseverance to cultivate and nurture it into existence. Some things will not just come to you; you have to labour and work through the process, but you grow through that process. There are some babies that will never be birthed unless you conceive, carry and nurture them into being, so go ahead and take the first step to conceive that baby. The path ahead will most certainly not be easy but if the baby is truly yours to carry and birth, then all obstacles will be surmounted and there will be joy, freedom and deliverance from circumstances that have held you back at that birthing.

I have gone through a life journey of ups and downs which has led to the maturation of my purpose. I have been called to the Mountain of family (as mentioned in Chapter 6). However, at the start of my journey with Cedarcube, I was not equipped to help families. I had to undertake a journey of learning on the job as it were, where I developed tools to help me go through the challenges I was facing in my own marriage and family. 2018 was a particularly difficult year when I was unemployed for almost 18 months. I was searching for my identity after my business partner had left the business the previous year. Our financial troubles in the family were further compounded by a series of unfortunate events.

However, in the midst of all this mess, I had several defining moments of enlightenment. It was at this downturn that God first started downloading to me the contents of this book and that I received the title, *The Awakening of Purpose Through Passion and Pain*. It was also at this time that I received a new vision for Cedarcube. Following a moment of meditation in the early hours of the morning, I received the mission of Healing Hearts and Strengthening Families as well as the four pillars on which the work was to be built; to Heal, Bond, Empower and Connect. I also started helping women who were suffering from domestic abuse and the Behind the Mask project was born. This led me to organise a successful masked charity fundraising gala that year.

Cedarcube started off as a lifestyle service for single and married Christians to bond with each other and connect and meet others. However, as time passed, I saw that families needed support with finances, parenting, communication, and in extreme cases, domestic abuse. I had to go through my own journey of struggling through communication and intimacy problems in my marriage, as well as financial challenges. These experiences gave me the tools to help me improve my outlook when life took a downturn, and to consciously change from a place of disruption to one of choice and hope.

In 2020, it seemed that a lot of the life experiences I had been undergoing up to that point culminated and started to make more sense. I had organised a summit in 2019 called

Building the Excellent Family which started very small with four speakers. By 2020, this had grown to 20 speakers, and it continues to grow from strength to strength. In that period in 2020, I had reached a breakthrough and was not only experiencing and growing in the pain, but mastering and graduating from it.

I also experienced some developments in my personal life; having had a strictly religious upbringing, my husband had been disillusioned by religion for several years and was somewhat angry with God. He concluded that religious leaders were deceptive, and that this indoctrination had robbed him of opportunities to experience life fully. In 2020, he caught the Covid-19 virus and was hospitalised from 23rd December to New Year's Eve. When he was discharged from hospital, he told us that on the worst night when he was fighting for his life, he had an epiphany that brought him closer to God. He was shown that all that mattered in life was love and that this should be unconditional. This experience brought him in closer alignment to his purpose and, in a way, mine too.

This was something that I had been praying for a long time; however, the time had not come for it to materialise until that moment. Some things take time and may yet not have happened because it is not the right time. You have to undergo the processing and the lessons and maturity attached to the experience to grow in it and master it. This is how true wisdom, knowledge, dominion and expertise in a given area occurs.

Purpose takes time and work! At this point, many become frustrated because they think walking in their purpose should be easy. You cannot leapfrog your way to success; you must go through the process and trust that if you are truly working (not only walking) in your purpose, the next step will be revealed, breakthrough will occur and, success will manifest at the right time.

The key is in the word 'process'. Anything processed takes work but when it's done, it is more refined and polished than before.

"For You, O God, have tested us; You have refined us as silver is refined." (Psalm 66:10)

Stop suffering from analysis paralysis – he who watches the wind never sows!

Is there something in your life that seems like an impossible task? What is it in your life that looks like an immovable mountain, which puts you off the work involved? Continue to persevere in tackling the task required to achieve your purpose because that is what will leave a legacy and ancient monument that people will admire for generations to come.

Prayers

- ◊ *"Lord, I need Your wisdom regarding my time management. Make me a wise manager of my time, and strengthen me to make choices that honor You, that lead me closer to You, and that reflect Your love to the world. Teach me to be intentional with the choices I make and the activities I'm involved in."* (https://praypedia.com/prayer/timemanagement.html)

- ◊ *"Oh God, help me to walk circumspectly, not as a fool but as a wise person, redeeming the time, because the days are evil. Therefore, Lord, help me not to be unwise, but to understand what your will for my life is."* (Ephesians 5:15-17)

◊ *"Oh God, teach me to number my days, so that I may apply my heart unto wisdom."* (Psalm 90:12)

Ihu's Proclamations

◊ I expect the unexpected, my glorious good now comes to pass.

◊ Now is the appointed time – today is the day of my amazing, good fortune.

◊ I always use my time wisely and intentionally on activities that contribute to the fulfilment of my purpose.

Ihu's Reflections

◊ Reflect on how you spend your time. Do you think you spend it well and intentionally on the things that contribute to the fulfilment of your purpose, such as developing your talents and skills or helping others, or not?

◊ Name three things you spend time on that distract your purpose.

◊ What actions are you going to take this week to ensure you starve your distractions and spend more time on purposeful activities?

CHAPTER NINE
Your Purpose Needs Money

"For which of you, intending to build a tower, does not sit down first and count the cost, whether he has enough to finish it."

(Luke 14:28-30)

Just as your purpose needs time, it also needs money to fund it. There is no great movement, mission or cause that did not require some sort of funding to flourish. Jesus' ministry was funded by wealthy philanthropists, often women who had benefited from his healing and teaching ministry.

Funding the gospel of Jesus Christ, or any other ministry, mission or project, requires a substantial amount of money. I am sure you have come across a free Bible in your hotel room when travelling. This gracious act is courtesy of the Gideons, formed by three Christian businessmen in 1898. By 1908 the organisation started placing Bibles in hotel rooms. Gideons International donated more than 1.4 million Bibles to hotels around the world between June 2018 and May 2019 alone. Of those, nearly 650,000 were in the

United States. Since then, the organisation has distributed more than 2.4 billion Bibles and today, their outreach goes worldwide to include military bases, schools and prisons.

You should protect, expect and respect money. Money flows freely; it goes where it is invited and stays where it is welcome. Unfortunately, many people waste their money because these funds are unattached and unassigned to a purpose. Just as your time needs to be given an assignment, your money also must be given an assignment.

Many people who eventually grow to have great wealth have been trained in the art of money management. This training has taken them through very difficult beginnings of abject struggle and poverty, or they had gone through the humbling process of making money and losing it several times over. Eventually, they often make even more money than before because through their losses, they had learnt the art of stewarding money correctly.

The Book of Job illustrates this story of loss and restoration very well. Job was tried and tested and lost everything: his children, his wife, his health and his source of livelihood. However, at the end of the story, he was rewarded with double what he had before, as he proved to be so faithful.

I also have my own story of loss and restoration. In 2013, I took a leap of faith by grabbing an opportunity to move into management. However, this meant a 90-minute commute as well as even more commuting within the job itself. This led to us moving home to be nearer my work. The toll of travel was still evident, even after moving closer to work, and I started suffering from chronic fatigue. I then had the opportunity of moving to another role in the city with less responsibility, less commute, but a lot more pay, and I took it. It was fine for a while but then this started a period of career downturns for me. Between 2014 and 2018, I lost a total of four jobs. I was given my notice in two jobs that were very good with excellent benefits in 2014 and 2016. And between September 2016 and October 2018, I didn't work at all.

2018 represented the crescendo of my downturn and that of our family as a whole. Our car fell into a ditch on 25th January as I was taking one of my sons to a birthday party, then on 27th January the same son suffered a hairline fracture on his foot whilst playing with his brothers.

Following that, I endured a painstaking period of months of taking three children to and from school on the bus, whilst one was on crutches, as we embarked on a three-month battle with the insurance company to give us a resolution to enable us to repair the old car or purchase a new one. I recall that winter being particularly cold and snowy. So, there I was, with no money, no car, taking three children to and from school daily on the bus, with one on crutches. It was difficult to see how it could get worse, but it did.

That same year, I had started helping in my brother's care business which had been started by my father prior to his death. There was some money coming in, though it was nowhere near what I was earning previously. Unfortunately, even that was short-lived because the business ended up being closed down that summer. In the same period, my husband underwent a five-hour surgery and had to rely heavily on my assistance and care.

To compound the difficulties, we had several household repairs that needed attention, such as a blocked drainage pipe. This meant that every time we washed up in the kitchen sink, we had to scoop the water up in a bucket to pour it out into the downstairs toilet. Using the dishwasher was out of the question because it was connected to the same drainage system so everything had to be washed by hand.

This experience made me lose attachments to money and the need to align my status and identity to my job title and how much money was in my pocket. From earning a good five-figure salary, I was now claiming government assistance; very humbling indeed.

However, at this time, my mission and purpose became clearer and more defined. I started a branch of Cedarcube helping women who had gone through domestic abuse and the mission to heal, bond, empower and connect families was borne. This was also the time that I received the inspiration for this book, as well as the blueprint of another book.

Now, after several years, things have turned around significantly; I am blessed with a six-figure income through my procurement consultancy and other businesses I run. The good thing is that through the experiences and suffering I had endured previously, I find that I have no attachment to this income. I see the income as a means to fulfil my purpose; I am aware that the reason I am a channel for it is due to the purpose it is being used for, so it does not stagnate or gets wasted at all.

Money is designed to flow – when it stops flowing, it stagnates. Do you ever wonder why it is that some people withhold money, yet do not prosper? Yet others are generous, but continue to grow and prosper? This is because money flows to those that will put it to good use.

The Book of Proverbs puts it perfectly:

"There is one who scatters yet increases more; And there is one who withholds more than is right, But it leads to poverty." (Proverbs 11:24)

Wealth can be built as a result of funding one's purpose, leading to sovereignty and the independence to make one's own choices. This is how real legacy can be attained. We are not simply building for the purpose at hand, but for our children, descendants and communities to come.

You waste money because your money is unassigned. So send your money on assignment and see it multiply!

Prayers

- ◊ *"Lord, help me trust You with my finances. Guide my decisions and help me to be wise with the resources You have given me. Show me how to manage my money in a way that honours You. Change my heart toward money and spending. Teach me to find contentment in You."* (10 Powerful Prayers for Your Finances, crosswalk.com)

- ◊ Lord, your word in Proverbs 21:20 says that *there is desirable treasure, And oil in the dwelling of the wise, But a foolish man squanders it.* Help me to be like the wise person who stewards treasure well and not like a fool who squanders it.

Ihu's Proclamations

- ◊ *"I am wealthy – God shall teach my hands to make wealth."* (Deuteronomy 8:18)
- ◊ *"I shall prosper even as my soul prospers."* (John 1:2)
- ◊ *"The plans of the diligent lead to profit, therefore all my plans lead to profit."* (Proverbs 21:5)
- ◊ My supply comes from God and big financial surprises now come to me in perfect ways under grace.

Ihu's Reflections

- ◊ What do you have to give?
- ◊ Givers never lack. Give and it shall be given unto you.
- ◊ Your time, money and talents help you to help others and contributes to the achievement of your purpose.
- ◊ What do you have to give?
- ◊ Reflect on how you have used the money given to you. Would you say you have been a good steward of this money or not?
- ◊ What steps can you take to steward your money better?

Chapter Ten
Your Purpose Needs People

"Since you were precious in My sight, You have been honoured, And I have loved you; Therefore I will give men for you, And people for your life."

(Isaiah 43:4)

Your purpose requires people. Whenever you step into your purpose, you will need people to help you to fulfil that purpose. They will come to you either by way of your recruitment or by attraction. Even Jesus recognised that he needed assistance as he recruited the 12 disciples who were men of various skills and abilities. Along the way, he had various followers, including many wealthy women such as Lydia and Mary Magdalene, who funded his ministry.

Many people make the mistake of trying to do everything by themselves. However, this is unsustainable and a recipe for burnout and discouragement. Building a team is vital to the long-term success and survival of your mission and purpose.

Team members can be placed in different categories:

1. **In-house team.** An in-house team is a team that you hire and pay to conduct work for you. This is a team of people that are central to the work that you do daily to make your mission work. They would typically take on the work you would have been doing yourself when starting off, such as administrative tasks.

2. **Outsourced team.** These are people who you would pay to manage a project for you, such as building a website, applying for a grant, conducting building works or marketing. In short, any area of expertise that someone has been trained to do and has more time and skill than you do.

3. **Partners.** These can be connected partners who act on your behalf and advocate for your work. They can also be partners based on goodwill, such as patrons or ambassadors, or they can be business partners or affiliates who work on certain projects with you for mutual benefit.

At some point in my business endeavours, I did everything myself; I was the social media manager, the website builder, the marketer, the campaign manager, etc. However, this was time-consuming, and I was unable to grow beyond a certain point so I had to invest in a team. I now have an in-house team that supports social media management and core administration, and the growth is evident. I am working on expanding even further as the demand for the work continues.

Aside from the above, there are people that don't necessarily work in the day-to-day operations of your business, or in any official capacity. However, they are your support network that allow you to be and do the best you are capable of. These people support you in the three key areas of your life: soul, physical and spiritual.

Your **soul** support system covers your emotional support, such as friends and family who help you in terms of providing a sounding board to give you advice, fun and social outlets that keep you whole and ensure that you are not constantly working. For instance, your partner or family members can provide domestic support with household chores and a loving base to come home to. Your partner can be a shoulder to cry on and be there to talk to and even provide back rubs when you have had a particularly difficult day. A good friend can provide emotional support by being a listening ear to vent to or a shoulder to cry on when things are not going quite as planned.

Your soul support system can include people that support you mentally, such as teachers, mentors and colleagues. These people have the skills and experience that you can call upon to make sound judgements in a certain area and they can advise you on the best way to achieve your goal.

Your **physical** support system can be people that help ensure that practical things are done. This can be a cleaner you pay to help with house chores, or it can be another parent from the school who helps pick up your children when you are engaged in other tasks or just to give you some rest time.

A **spiritual** support system can be people who pray for you and with you, or a church that you attend to find spiritual solace on a regular basis. It can be a spiritually mature friend or guide who helps provide you with insight or confirms a spiritual insight that you have already received.

Over the years, I have established a good emotional support system in my family and friends who know of my mission and are there to provide love, physical support and guidance.

I know very well the importance of spiritual support and I have built spiritual mentors around me whom I communicate very closely and regularly with, and who help support and guide me. I have a very close relationship with my local church, and they are aware of what I do and provide support where possible. In addition, I have friends who are a source of mutual spiritual support.

In order to hire a team or build a support network around you, you need to develop good skills in human relations. You need to ask yourself the following questions:

1. **Professional relationships**. How do you relate to other people? Do you play well with others? Do you connect with others? Are you showing up as a leader that other people want to support? How do you show up from a place of service? Remember, the universe is more responsive to work that is of service to humanity rather than serving your purpose alone. Professional relationships allow you to extend and expand your reach in a way that allows your businesses and mission to be global.

2. **Intimate relationships**. This area covers sexuality, which is a direct pathway to your parasympathetic nervous system, conducive for creation and, in essence, your divinity. It is essential for your mission and your purpose to ensure your intimate relationships are healthy and supportive, rather than in fight or flight mode which is akin to the sympathetic nervous system, and unconducive to growth and creativity.

3. **Family dynamics and relationships.** What experiences from your childhood are triggering you or disempowering you to now have successful relationships? You need to be able to take your inner child along and address issues so that you can lead from a place of emotional maturity. Invest in therapy if necessary to heal any of these issues that may be blocking your progress and stopping you from developing successful relationships in adulthood.

4. **Executive presence and communication.** What is your capacity to magnetise what you want and need? The most powerful leaders are not usually the most talkative but when they talk, people listen; they are magnetic. They are comfortable in their experience and skills drawn from different backgrounds and acquired and honed over the years.

You need to invest in the ability to communicate effectively. Different people have their parts to play in your life; however, you must step up and step out in your mission and purpose before they can appear. As the saying goes, "When the student is ready, the teacher appears". However, I say, "When the leader is ready, their followers and tribe appears." The move always starts with you.

Something to take note of is an irrational dislike of someone, especially when the relationship has gone smoothly beforehand. This is something I have experienced! I got connected to a wonderful lady in the education sector who was prolific at building networks. I subsequently invited her to speak at one of my summits. I engaged her in providing a service to help my children access private schools, a service which I paid a substantial amount for. However, the service delivery did not go according to plan,. Furthermore, I felt that there was no real aftercare around the service provided. She started networking events for Christian women which I had the opportunity to attend. I could have let my recent sour experience discourage me from having anything to do with her or any of her services, but I decided to attend one of them. This proved to be a very valuable experience because through her network, I met a number of great connections. One of them facilitated a one-week work experience for my son at Bloomberg as well as attended a couple of my own events, and two others became speakers at my event.

The point here is to look beyond emotions and ask yourself, *How can this connection be of benefit to my purpose and that of others?*

I am a strong believer that our calling and purpose is for a set time, a time when everything in the universe appears to bring it to its ultimate glorious and perfect fruition. When we delay our mission and know we should have stepped out several seasons ago, we delay the impact that mission would have had, had it been executed at the time it was given. I believe that when people appear in your life who you know are supposed to be useful and want to help you, but you can't find a need for them yet, they may have been assigned to you in a period when you failed to take action at the time required causing that mission to become overdue or even worse, defunct.

Prayers

◊ Oh God, cause Angels of light to move at the speed of light to make divine alignments and introductions that will benefit my purpose and vision.

- ◊ Lord, send me my destiny helpers speedily.
- ◊ Oh God, remove from me anyone who is there to distract, detract from or kill steal or destroy my purpose.

Ihu's Proclamations

- ◊ Every step I take is bringing me closer to the right people to successfully achieve my divine purpose.
- ◊ I shall not be unequally yoked with people that will detract from my purpose.
- ◊ I choose the people I work with, by wisdom and discernment.

Ihu's Reflections

- ◊ Reflect on the work you're doing. Which area do you think you would need most help in right now?
- ◊ How would this help make a difference in the fulfilment of your purpose?
- ◊ What steps would you be taking this week to ensure you get the help that you need?

Chapter Eleven
Single on Purpose

"He who is unmarried cares for the things of the Lord – how he may please the Lord. But he who is married cares about the things of the world – how he may please his wife"

(1 Corinthians 7:32-33)

If possible, it is advisable to discover and start walking in your purpose when you are single. Purpose takes time, energy, effort and money, and these resources are more readily available when single.

As a single person, your time is solely yours, but when married with children, quality time must be allocated to your spouse to help build a successful marriage, and to children to raise them to become fully equipped adults capable of pursuing their own purpose. Purpose can be demanding of time – for instance, you may be required to travel often to speak or to minister, or attend trainings, meetings and networking events. When you are single, you don't have to consult or agree with anyone else, and you don't have to inform a significant other of your decisions.

However, as a married person, your partner should be informed and consulted in decisions, and schedules would need to be coordinated and agreed. Some situations concerning the development and progression of your purpose may require very quick decisions – this is much easier as a single person because you only have yourself to consider. When married, however, consultation and agreement with your partner is very important and is the very key to a successful partnership. At the same time, this may mean that many opportunities are foregone due to the time taken to make the decision – that is if your spouse even agrees to it!

When purpose is being pursued whilst also married with a family, you must work twice as hard because your actions no longer affect only you. However, if you are in the throes of pursuing your purpose when you meet your partner, then the partner is fully aligned with your purpose and possibly willing to be a co-labourer for its fruitful fulfilment.

Marriage is full of challenges as two different individuals with two completely different, sometimes polarised, upbringings, traits and characters merge to become one unit. The process of merging is not always a smooth one and when one partner introduces a new life pursuit that demands money and time away from the home, as well as additional support, it may not be an easy thing to assimilate.

In accordance with the Law of Attraction, 'like attracts like' or you may attract a partner who is the missing piece to the puzzle you need to bring your purpose to a successful and fruitful realisation. When you are already walking in your purpose, you will attract and be surrounded by those who carry the right skills and resources to help you fulfil it. I strongly believe that many people end up with the wrong spouse because they have delayed starting on the path of purpose that God has laid out for them, causing them to attract the wrong person in their life. So, for me, the priority is always purpose first, marriage second!

I was blessed to have received the vision to start a Christian lifestyle organisation when I was single. I dedicated all my time, efforts and money to this cause without challenge from anyone. I was able to organise a launch event which cost approximately £2,500 at the time, as well as a retreat.

It is very likely that you will end up meeting your life partner in the very process of working out your purpose. As God is a kind God, when you are walking the path that He has laid out for you, He will bring you a partner who at the very least understands your purpose and will not circumvent it in any way, and at the very best will work together with you towards its fulfilment. This is illustrated by Ruth's story in the Bible. Ruth met Boaz as she busied herself in the threshing field. Note two key points; one, she was out in the field and not at home, and two, she wasn't found idle. She busied herself with the work presented before her.

"But seek first the kingdom of God and His righteousness, and all these things shall be added to you." (Matthew 6:33)

I met my partner in a similar way. I was in the process of pursuing my purpose, not knowing that the field contained my marital future even though I wasn't searching for it! God proved His word that if we seek ye first the kingdom of God, all these things shall be added unto us.

My experience with my husband has very much driven the direction and development of my vision. As I went through my own experiences, it helped me to know first hand the type of help that couples and families needed. Prior to my marriage, my vision was one-dimensional, focused on singles. With my broader marital experience, I now understood that couples also needed even more help after they got married, and in sustaining their relationship, managing finances and raising children. The marriage isn't simply about the couple, but about the next generation and even generations to come. I can say that my marriage was a training ground to enable me to serve better in my purpose.

Being single is an important time to understand who you are and where your talents, skills and abilities lie. This knowledge will help you understand who and what you are looking for in friendships and marriage.

Covenant relationships are relationships that seem predestined and are of mutual benefit to your purpose. They are marked by a very strong bond which can sometimes be instantaneous. The type of friendship that David and Jonathan from the Book of Samuel in the Bible had is a good example of such a relationship. Here is a guide to help you recognise covenant relationships so that you don't risk getting into false relationships that will divert your purpose, frustrate you and waste your time.

1. **You are not unequally yoked (2 Corinthians 6:14).** Yoked together means being connected and bonded through experience or a common goal that binds you together. It could even be through a formal agreement such as a contract. In true covenant relationships, there is always a balance where one complements or completes the other, creating perfect harmony. The burdens that both parties carry are usually equal. You may have different personalities, but you are roughly of the same calibre in all areas that matter, intellectually and spiritually.

2. **Iron sharpens Iron (Proverbs 27:17).** This means that you both make each other better, driving one another to become the best that you can be. You can identify covenant partners because you make each other sharper and more potent, bringing out the best in each other. Covenant partnerships are therefore relationships of mutual benefit and reciprocity.

3. **A man sharpens the countenance of his friend (Proverbs 27:17).** A covenant friend has a way of cheering you up when you are feeling low. You both have a way of sharpening each other's countenance. You make each other laugh and smile and you look forward to being in each other's company because the high joyful energy and spirits of one friend or partner lifts up the spirits of the other.

4. **You are kindred spirits (A friend that sticks closer than a brother, Proverbs 18:24).** One of the key indicators that you have a covenant relationship is that you both feel very comfortable with each other. You could talk for hours on end or feel equally comfortable sitting in silence. Distance or time is not an issue because no matter how far away you are, you are emotionally in tune with each other. No matter how long you go without talking, whenever you reconnect, you pick up where you left off. You are comfortable in each other's company and whenever you reconnect, it's as if you've come home.

5. **You make a formidable partnership.** A covenant relationship can be marked by its fruitfulness. There are relationships that bring about extraordinary multiplication and one of the remarkable things about these relationships is the speed that success

manifests itself. They are marked by unity which is a perfect environment for success to occur very quickly. These relationships are evidence that there is power in unity.

6. **Your relationship stands the test of time.** A key mark of a covenant relationship is that they have longevity. Though they may go through several trials like others and sometimes even more so, they come out stronger on the other side. Covenant relationships are marked by much forgiveness and an unconditional love that causes them to stand the test of time.

I wish for you that you truly find alliances and relationships that are covenant relationships so that you and your purpose can be elevated by these unique connections.

Prayers

◊ Oh God, position me in the right ground and environment that will enable my purpose to thrive.

◊ God, send me true covenant relationships that will support and enhance your purpose for my life.

◊ God, help me to discern and remove from me all relationships that are counterfeit diverters and detractors of my destiny in Jesus.

Ihu's Proclamations

- ◊ I am a gentle, kind, loving and generous person.
- ◊ I have all the qualities of a good friend or partner.
- ◊ I am able to form good, long-lasting covenant relationships.
- ◊ I am healed from relationships that did not serve me in the past. I am wiser now and able to make better choices in my future relationships. I will not repeat the same mistakes.

Ihu's Reflections

- ◊ Take a moment to reflect on your qualities; what qualities make you a good friend?
- ◊ Reflect on your previous relationships. What went wrong and how will you avoid these mistakes in the future?
- ◊ What did you like about your past relationships and how will you bring these qualities to your new relationships?
- ◊ Reflect on your friendships. What qualities represent a good friend? How would you like this relationship to be?
- ◊ Reflect on your romantic relationships. What qualities would you like to see in your significant other? How would you like this relationship to be?

Chapter Twelve
The Purpose-Aligned Marriage

"And the Lord God said, 'It is not good that man should be alone; I will make him a helper comparable to him.'"

(Genesis 2:18)

You will often find that when you are walking in your purpose, the path often leads you to your life partner, because you are walking in the path that God has laid out for you since the beginning of time.

This was certainly my experience. Many people have heard me say that it was through researching and working on implementing the vision God had given me for Cedarcube, that I found my husband – or rather he found me!

When I first started Cedarcube, it was to be a lifestyle service for single Christians, providing a fellowship where they could socialise with those of like-mind without having to resort to attending nightclubs. Part of the service was to create a vetted online dating site. One had to enter details on the profile form to be able to move to the next stage, so I entered basic information without adding a profile picture – to my surprise, I started being contacted by men looking for a partner. I ignored most of them but one was particularly persistent! I remember thinking "How can he be that persistent even without seeing my photo yet?!" He eventually sent me a poem that caught my attention, that was about me being the bone of his bone and the flesh of his flesh. After that, I called him and the rest, as they say, is history!

Hearing the story from my husband Chidi's perspective is even more profound. At that point, he had only been in the country for a year, living with his brother and sister-in-law. He had recently moved into his own place, one bedroom in a house of multiple occupancy. He wanted to meet a partner and was advised to join a Christian dating site by a friend in church. He had never used a computer in his life! Mind you, this was in 2002 and not everyone was as familiar with the internet and PCs then. He asked his brother to help him purchase a computer.

When it was all set up, one of the first things he did was to join a dating site, hence his interaction with me. In hindsight, it seems that the sole purpose the universe had for him to buy the computer was to meet me! Had I not been diligent in pursing that assignment of registering on the website for my purpose, we would have missed each other. Call it coincidence? I think not! I call it divine synchronicity, which can only occur if you step into your right purpose at the right time and if you obey the gentle nudges from your divine source to take strategic actions at specific times which are all tied to your purpose.

When choosing a life partner once you have already started on the path to your purpose, it is vital that you insightfully choose a partner that will labour with you. Do not be unequally 'yoked' because like two unbalanced mules, the wrong partner can hinder your path and slow you down. Indeed, many have sabotaged the progress of their purpose as a result of making the wrong choice of life partner. This affliction seems to affect women more adversely than men due to the patriarchal structure of modern societies that deems that a woman's place is in the home and that her main purpose after marriage is to serve and nurture her husband and children. Many men truly embed these views in the wrong way, stifling the growth and progress of their wives.

Conversely, choosing the right partner can multiply and enhance your efforts. Indeed, *"one person can chase one thousand but two can chase ten thousand"* (Deuteronomy 32:30). It is therefore clear that there is a special acceleration that comes with a union made in agreement and there is no better example of such a union than that of marriage.

The enemy knows this truth and uses the institution of marriage to trap so many into bondage and lives of pain and unfulfilled potential. Nothing will grow in a toxic environment even if unity commands the blessing.

"Behold, how good and how pleasant it is for brethren to dwell together in unity! It is like the dew of Hermon, descending upon the mountains of Zion; For there the Lord commanded the blessing – Life forevermore." (Psalm 133:1)

Your own limiting beliefs and mindset can also stop you from being all that you were created to be. Many women embed the societal views that once they get married, then their career or grand aspirations they once had are over.

If you are such a woman reading this, then I am here to persuade you that God does not make mistakes; you are created with your own unique gifts, talents and abilities in the body of a woman for a specific purpose and time as this. You can still be a wife and a mother **and** fulfil your purpose. In fact, when women are truly walking in their purpose, due to their more empathetic and nurturing natures, they tend to benefit their communities and more people in general. This has been proven in research such as that summarised in an article by Aisha Dabi, 'Women are the key to economic development in third-world countries'.

So woman – stop waiting… the world needs you!

Many women struggle to get 'buy in' from their partners to walk fully in their purpose. I have experienced this myself when my partner did not see the relevance or importance of my continuing in my mission for Cedarcube, especially when it seemed that my efforts were not bearing fruit. If this is you, then I would ask you to persevere! Walking in your purpose and obtaining 'buy in' from people dear to you can often be difficult and is not always a given. However, you will win if you persevere; your partner and everyone else will have no choice but to come on side when they see your determination and focus when it comes to achieving your goals.

Prayers

- ◊ Oh God, you said in Proverbs 21:1 *"that the King's heart is in your hands to turn whichever way You choose"* so please turn my partner's heart towards you, my mission, and my purpose.

- ◊ Oh God, you said in Proverbs 10:22 *"that your blessings maketh rich and your add no sorrow to it,"* therefore I pray that my marriage will forever bring me joy, bringing us to a prosperous place that

◊ benefits our purpose and there will be no sorrow in it.

◊ In Psalm 84:11, you say *"for the LORD God is a sun and shield; The LORD will give grace and glory; No good thing will He withhold From those who walk uprightly,"* therefore according to your word Lord, I pray that all the goodness that lies in marriage shall not be withheld from me.

Ihu's Proclamations

◊ *"I have a happy marriage, home and family – we shall dwell together in harmony and our unity shall command the blessing and life forevermore."* (Psalm 133:1)

◊ *"My children rise up and call me blessed; My husband also calls me blessed and he praises me."* (Proverbs 31:28)

◊ *"My home is built in wisdom, in understanding it is established; By knowledge the rooms are filled with all precious and pleasant riches."* (Proverbs 24:3-4)

Ihu's Reflections

If you have found it challenging obtaining agreement or understanding from your partner in pursuing your purpose, then follow these simple but effective steps which have also worked for me:

◊ Reflecting on your marriage, can you identify its purpose?

- Reflecting on a time you and your spouse achieved something great, what steps did you take to get there?

- Reflecting on a time that things did not go so well in something that you planned in your marriage, what caused the failure or disagreement?

- What steps will you take in the future to ensure that your spouse is brought on side in the decisions you make in your marriage?

Chapter Thirteen
Developing Purpose in Children

*"Train up a child in the way he should go,
And when he is old he will not depart from it."*

(Proverbs 22:6)

I find that it always helps to instil in children a sense of what their purpose is early in life. As a parent, you are a mentor, a guide and a steward to your child. If you are paying attention, you will find that the divine source has given you an insight into what your child's gifts are. Giftings are more evident and authentic the closer a soul is to their birth, so therefore it is of utmost importance as a parent to watch and observe the natural inclinations of your children when they are infants and toddlers, preferably before the age of five. Do they like kicking a ball around? Are they empathetic? Do they have wit? Do they have a great singing voice and affinity with music? Do they like to put on a show and be centre stage? These are the traits you can observe in your child to give an indication of where you should focus your efforts and investment to help them develop their natural gifts and talents.

As mentioned before, for me, it was in fashion. I would always design and sketch dresses, particularly wedding dresses. If I couldn't find a piece of clothing or accessory in the shop, I would buy the fabric to make it myself!

Without discipline, guidance and a dose of self-confidence, many natural gifts would not develop into the fullness of what God had intended, causing their owner to fall short of walking in the fullness of their purpose and perhaps languishing in obscurity as a result.

I have a dear childhood friend who has always been an avid reader; she would rather skip mealtimes than miss out on finishing a chapter! She also writes effortlessly.

She has shared many wonderful literary works with me and others close to her; however, to our dismay, she is yet to publish any of her works.

Every great gift requires a parent, teacher or mentor who is determined to bring out those gifts.

A formal cultural consensus analysis of responses on when parents can best influence their children, found strong agreement that the greatest impact of parenting on a child's development occurs at adolescence, at around 12 years old. ('When can parents most influence their child's development?' Worthman, Tomlinson & Rotheram-Borus)

According to several worldwide studies including 'The Best Start for Life, A Vision for the 1001 Critical Days', a study conducted by Early Years Healthy Development Review, the most important time to influence a child's development is from birth to two years old. These studies highlight that parents that exercised their authority, with clearly defined behavioural expectations and boundaries, tend to raise confident and independent children. By contrast, children raised by uninvolved and overly liberal parents may struggle to regulate their emotions and tend to develop unhealthy social relationships.

We have heard great stories of sacrifice about children whose parents have obsessively nurtured the talent of their children to greatness. They sacrificed a 'normal' childhood for hours of practice. However, this was the price they paid for their greatness and success. We know that The Jackson 5 had an extremely disciplinarian father in Joe Jackson. Though Michael was the most famous of them all, followed by his sister Janet, the family legacy of The Jackson 5 and their hits still live on. Some would argue that Michael Jackson and his siblings were greatly damaged by their upbringing, with Michael never growing up and becoming very much a Peter Pan character, living the childhood he never had, as a grown man in an adult body. However, the question is, if their childhoods had been ordinary, would they have been the extraordinary adult stars we know today?

Let's move to Richard Williams, the father, coach and manager of arguably two of the greatest female tennis players of all time, Venus and Serena Williams. He became infatuated with the game of tennis, having never played it in his life. After watching a game where he witnessed a coach hand over $40,000 cheque to a 25-year-old player, he said to himself, *I am going to have two kids and get them into tennis.* Unbelievably, he knew what the purpose of his children would be before they were even conceived! He visualised his children playing and being great at tennis before they were born! His life and legacy were encapsulated in a film, *King Richard*, where we see a father guiding two of his daughters to greatness with absolute determination, and huge attention to detail; he even wrote a 78-page plan detailing how he would nurture their talents to success!

Richard did whatever he could to ensure his daughters succeeded; he took them to tennis camps, hired coaches and even built a tennis court in their backyard. All this shows the crucial role of parents in giving birth to the purpose of their children and helping them to become all that they can be.

The Richard Williams of this world show us clearly that we are not mere observers in our lives and in the lives of the things we create. We are active creators made in the image and likeness of God and we can actively shape and mould our lives as well as the lives of our children into what we want. As parents, we have authority over our children and we can ethically nurture them into their highest selves, not in a selfish way to live a life we didn't live, but in a sacrificial and knowledgeable way, guiding them into becoming the best that God intended and purposed them to be.

Prayers

- ◊ Oh God, help me to perceive and understand the giftings you have deposited in my children.

- ◊ Oh God, equip me with all that I need to raise my children and bring out their giftings so that they can fulfil their purpose.

Ihu's Proclamations

- ◊ My children shall be recipients of generational blessings.

- ◊ *"Behold, children are a heritage from the Lord, the fruit of my womb a reward. Like arrows in the hand of a warrior are the children of my youth. Blessed am I who fills my quiver with them!"* (Psalm 127:3)

- ◊ *"All my children shall be taught by the Lord and great shall be the peace of my children."* (Isaiah 54:13)

- ◊ My children shall fulfil their purposes on Earth.

Ihu's Reflections

- ◊ What giftings do you observe in your children?
- ◊ In what ways can you give purpose to your children to help them become all that they can be?

Chapter Fourteen
Overcoming Satanic Opposition - My Story

*"Many are the afflictions of the righteous,
But the Lord delivers him out of them all."*

(Psalm 34:19)

Your path to purpose will not necessarily be smooth sailing. There will be several oppositions along the way, but you must push past and overcome them. Opposition can take many different forms.

External negative forces

We have all been put on Earth to use our passion or pain to achieve a purpose. We have already explored our tripartite nature, body, soul and spirit in previous chapters, and just as there are physical and spiritual resources put in our way to help us achieve our purpose, there are also malevolent forces at play to thwart these efforts.

To aid understanding and for simplicity, I will call these forces Satanic attacks. Satanic attacks can come in the form of unexplained obstacles and battles that go beyond the normal ups and downs of life, especially when they seem to occur in repetitive cycles.

Like most people, I have faced some disappointments in my life, but I would say that my story is very much one of 'displacement', just like Esther in the Bible.

Esther was a young Jewish girl but she was 'displaced' when she became an orphan and a refugee in the Persian city of Susa. Originally known as Hadassah, Esther was adopted by her cousin, Mordecai. She became Queen of Persia to the Emperor Ahasuerus (loosely based on Xerxes, 485-464 BC). The Emperor's evil minister, Haman, pursued a vendetta against the Jews, by issuing a royal decree ordering their destruction. Esther's influence and intervention thwarts the vengeance of Haman and saves the Jewish people from destruction. Esther was placed in an influential position as Queen, "for such a time as this". God's purpose was therefore accomplished through Esther.

Esther's story of early displacement and adversity shows that your beginning does not determine your end. You can still fulfil your purpose and achieve greatness even if your beginning was humble or even difficult.

One of my earliest disappointments was at the age of 10, after I had taken the Nigerian Common Entrance Exam to access secondary school. I really wanted to join my sister at the Federal Government Girls School in Owerri.

I had received information that I had passed the exam but when my mother and I went to check the results, my name was not on the list. I had been removed along with four other girls and replaced with indigenes from the northern states of Nigeria.

This sort of fraud was common and I had now fallen victim to it. I ended up attending the less desirable state secondary school, Owerri Girls School. The buildings and equipment were dilapidated, and the food was nothing to write home about. I developed anaemia and my mum had to take me out of the school after one term. I would say, however, that being in the secondary school rather than Federal Government Girls College made the decision for me to come to the UK easier.

Later that year in the summer of 1988, my mother, brothers and I joined my father in the UK. It was supposed to be a summer holiday, but it ended up being a permanent stay. My dad had left Nigeria two years prior as a result of his involvement in politics; he had been caught up in the political coup of 1986 where the civilian government had been overthrown, just as he was about to be installed into the House of Senate as a Senator. Our lives would have been so different had that success not been so short-lived. Instead, I was thrown into a different world in the UK, far from all that I knew and loved. I was amazed to see that it was still daylight at 8 pm!

However, prior to coming to the UK, a self-inflicted accident meant my hair had to be shaved off completely, making me look like a boy. All the stares I received further compounded my discomfort at being in a strange land.

My mother did not want to stay in the UK as she had a very influential job as an Area Manager in one of the big four Nigerian banks at the time. She went back home to her job and my older sister who was still at school in Nigeria, leaving three of us in the UK; me at aged eleven, and two younger brothers, aged eight and four. As I reflect at the great sacrifice my mother made leaving her young family behind, I can't help but think that she must have been heartbroken having to make that difficult decision.

A bed and breakfast facing Finsbury Park in North London became our home. Robbed of my rite of passage into adulthood, I became mother to my brothers as my father spent most of his time working as a taxi driver to make ends meet, even though he was an Oxford trained medical doctor. With uncanny resilience, I accepted this new reality as my truth and norm.

My new reality was the opposite of my innocent, happy, carefree and somewhat privileged existence as a young girl in Nigeria, in a home surrounded by house helps. I would have sand and water fights with neighbours or climb up the mango tree in front of our vast and exotic fruit tree-laden yard to get lost in a book. We went from the hustle and excitement of a typical morning consisting of one of my dad's drivers dropping us off to school on the political campaign bus, the megaphone blasting *Vote Dr Obi Nwagwu, Vote the Action Doctor*! and a home being surrounded by supporters and campaign managers, to our new stark reality in London.

Most evenings involved me coming down to the communal kitchen with our big pot to make dinner, whilst my eight-year-old brother washed up in the small sink in our bedroom afterwards. I would read them bedtime stories before continuing my own homework and then going to bed. I was often late for school as I found it difficult juggling all my chores and would leave chores like ironing my uniform until the morning. On Saturdays, my dad would give us about £20 so that we could go shopping while he went to work.

One of the highlights of my early years in London was a friendship with an Irish girl called Deidre Reilly. We became the best of friends, and her family became my second family. They lived on the Caledonian Road (so not far from me) and we used to all go swimming together most Saturdays. We even went to a theme park together with her family. I felt that I had found solace, a stable family unit where I could simply be a girl and have fun again. If I'm being honest, I also took a fancy to her older brother who looked like a young Tom Cruise, muscles and all!

However, life dealt me a crushing blow, again! Deidre and her family suddenly returned to Ireland. It was as if the rug had been pulled once again from under my feet – my joy and security blanket was gone. I had no friends and school became a lonely, cruel and torturous place. The playground exposed my lack of friends, so every day, I chose to eat my lunch hiding inside the toilets on the fourth floor. I was also bullied by a group of girls due to having cropped hair and looking like a boy, a legacy from when I had arrived from Nigeria which did not help me assimilate into my new surroundings.

The bullying continued when I moved schools after my mum and sister joined us in the UK in 1990. From the bed and breakfast in Finsbury Park, we moved to Edmonton, further towards north-east London, where we got a new council flat. Though an upgrade from the bed and breakfast, the new accommodation was still a huge drop in the standard of lifestyle we had been accustomed to in Nigeria as a family; my mother made the sacrifice to leave her bank manager job to start again, doing menial cleaning jobs whilst my father continued driving taxis.

However, in the midst of it all, fortune smiled at me once again as I had made a new best friend, a bubbly and popular Ghanaian girl called Sheila, and I had become bolder and happier. Afternoons after school would be spent at Sheila's house dressing up and dancing to hip-hop videos. We also had a wider group of about four other friends and I regularly used to go out with my sister and her friends as my sister had quickly befriended some of the popular girls in her year. I finally started enjoying young teenage life!

From our council flat, we received an offer to buy a property; my dad, having great aspirations, chose to buy a place in the affluent suburb of Loughton by Epping Forest in Essex. We became part of and involved in a wider ethnic and migrant, expatriate community.

My adolescent experience carried on into young adulthood as I was offered a place to study economics at the University of Bradford. This was probably the most enjoyable time of my experience so thus far in the UK. I displayed strong organisational and leadership skills as I became the social secretary for a newly resurrected African Caribbean Society. I managed to get the organisation out of debt and in the black by spearheading various paid events. This was a remarkable time in my life – I enjoyed my life as a budding young adult, making many lasting friendships along the way.

I went on to study a Master's degree in information technology and was working part-time at an internet service provider as a customer service agent. Whilst studying for my Master's degree, I experienced my first serious relationship. It was a multi-racial relationship with a young man who used to work in the same company as a marketing director. We dated for two and a half years during which time I completed my degree and had started working full-time. Life was good for a while as I enjoyed work in the bubbly advertising sector, working for the BBC and then at a top advertising firm, Ogilvy & Mather. I was fending for myself and learning about independent living as I moved in close to my boyfriend in a shared accommodation with new friends. We became engaged but he was non-committal.

Life took another downturn as I got made redundant shortly after we became engaged. I was unemployed for a while, and I tried my hand at developing my own company but struggled. In the midst of this, I felt there was something missing in my life, and I began seeking for the missing piece. My search directed me to a newspaper called *The Voice* and subsequently to a church consequently located a stone's throw from where the bed and breakfast we used to live in, across the road from Finsbury Park. I walked into an electric atmosphere where prayers were being made and sat down in bemusement as this was something I had never seen before or was used to, even though I had grown up in a Catholic home. The Pastor was led to pray for me and I found myself having an out-of-body experience.

As he laid hands on me, he mentioned seeing that someone had used a picture of me and laid a curse that rendered it difficult for me to succeed financially and to be happily married. I was crying and screaming. I knew I was doing this but at the same time it felt as if I was an observer in the whole process.

This was a defining moment in my life as I received spiritual deliverance and an impartation from God. This felt like I had received a completely new spirit within me, a new way of seeing the world. I felt that there was an inner guide in me leading me to do things in a different way. I felt a presence, as if I was being led to make drastic changes to a life that now seemed completely alien to me. I suddenly felt awakened.

From then on, my life changed. I decided to break off with my boyfriend and move back home. My sister introduced me to her church and I made new friends there. I continued to grow in my new-found passion and spirituality, often socialising and fellowshipping with my new Christian friends. I took on several jobs, including working for my father.

On Sundays, I would normally go to church and to a house fellowship on Wednesdays. I even started helping out in different church departments such as children's church. One Sunday I didn't go to church as usual, and I was praying in my room. That day I received something called the Baptism of the Holy Spirit or the ability to speak in different tongues and I ended up praying in an unknown language. I was in this state for at least five hours, but I didn't realise how much time had passed as this seemed to be another out-of-body experience!

During this period, I received the vision in a dream to start Cedarcube, leading to me meeting my husband as previously mentioned. Though it was love at first sight when we met and we were fully convinced that we wanted to spend the rest of our lives together, as a married Christian, I found myself experiencing a plethora of different battles.

One of them started whilst we were courting with my father not wanting us to marry to the extent that he said if we got married and he died that we should not attend his funeral! His dislike for my husband was so great that when we travelled to Nigeria, Chidi would call and if my dad picked up the phone, he would rain abuse on him and slam the phone down!

So many strange things happened whilst we were engaged. For instance, I dreamt that my engagement ring was stolen by a strange creature and then I woke up to find the ring missing. A close member of Chidi's family, one of his brothers' wives, took a dislike to me which spilled over into our marriage. She loathed me for no reason whatsoever and I later found out that she was upset that Chidi chose me and not someone else she had recommended for him.

Chidi and I decided to embark on a 21-day prayer and fasting session and were able to overcome the storms surrounding our marriage through the power of unity and faith. On the last day of the fast, it was also the day we were returning from a retreat I had organised through Cedarcube for singles. The universe conspired to bring together my aunty from Nigeria and my brother, two people my father held in deep respect, along with my mother. They were all in the house upon our return from our long weekend retreat.

The conversation turned to my marital plans, and everyone present proceeded to plead my case with my father to give his consent for us to marry. He eventually gave in that same day and decided to grant his consent for the marriage to proceed. I knelt in front of him as he gave me his blessing. A few months after that, when Chidi's family came to 'knock for me' which meant to formally ask for my hand in marriage as tradition demanded, my dad then gave both of us his blessing, as we knelt before him.

In May 2005, the two families were finally united, and we had a glorious 'society' wedding of close to 300 guests in Loughton, UK. I am so pleased we did because my father passed away on 28th December of that same year from cancer of the pancreas. I had prophetically foreseen his death in two recurring dreams prior to his diagnosis in July of the same year.

Upon marriage, we rented a two-bedroom house in Thamesmead, nearer Chidi, and we eventually bought our own place. The early years of marriage were reasonably happy; we had three sons in quick succession, and after seven years in south-east London, we moved back to the leafier suburbs of Loughton in 2013. We used the opportunity of getting closer to my new job in Hertfordshire to get away from the potential challenges of raising a young family in the city. Marriage, however, became tough as we faced periods of financial turbulence and challenges in our relationship.

As mentioned, the period between 2014 and 2018 were particularly difficult; remember, I lost a total of four jobs. We had several disappointments as I often lost my job just before we were about to get our mortgage approved. I felt that my finances were under attack by an unseen malevolent force.

The frustration and instability took its toll on our marriage as we argued constantly. Even in the midst of this, I had an 'Aha!' moment – I realised that by experiencing these painful episodes, I may have been in training to help others that would go through these difficulties themselves. It was all part of the fulfilment of my purpose – if I could help myself, I could also help others! The experience taught me tools to help myself, to consciously change from a place of disruption to one of choice, and placed me in a position to be able to help others.

Satanic opposition can come in the form of word curses

"Death and life are in the power of the tongue, And those who love it will eat its fruit." (Proverbs 18:21)

I am a strong believer that the words we speak carry power that can either be creative or destructive. Just as the Earth was created through words, we humans that are made in the image of God, the infinite source of all things, also have this power. This is why you should be very mindful of the confessions (also known as affirmations) you make, because you confirm life situations both positive and negative through the words that you constantly affirm. The confessions or affirmations you make knowingly or unknowingly, as well as those that are made over you by others, are watered by your thoughts, fears and emotions which compound to create your realities.

Even Jesus encouraged the weak to say *I am strong* and the poor to say *I am rich*. Your pronouncements make all the difference in creating your reality. If your today is not appealing, you can speak to the atmosphere to create a better tomorrow. Do not go by what you see but what you perceive. The righteous indeed shall live by faith!

Much reverence is given to ministers of God as authority figures and rightly so. However, it is important to note that you too have a level of authority, and don't always have to go to someone else to make pronouncements over you through prayer. In fact, you must do this with great caution and test all spirits before you give others the access and permission to speak into your lives. Our mouths are gateways that should not be taken lightly. We should be particularly weary of the effect of the words spoken about and over us by authority figures due to their elevated influence. Many people's self-confidence have been destroyed because of the effects of a negative word, spoken by a parent, a teacher or a spiritual leader such as a priest. These words can take root in the subconscious psyche and go on to manifest into a mind stronghold which can work to divert your God-given destiny.

"Many will say to Me in that day, 'Lord, Lord, have we not prophesied in Your name, cast out demons in Your name, and done many wonders in Your name?' And then I will declare to them, 'I never knew you; depart from Me, you who practice lawlessness!" (Matthew 7:22-23)

The enemy has indeed infiltrated the church system and perverted the word of God so that it is used as a weapon of oppression to blind people and rob them of their destinies, as opposed to setting them free. The enemy has come masked as an angel of light. Remember that Lucifer was an angel in heaven, blessed with many desirable qualities before his fall from grace. The enemy uses deception to thwart people from walking in their missions and callings and to steal their joy which is crucial to creativity.

Our own fear can be a barrier

There is a well-known saying that what we focus on grows. It is evident that in life we attract what we fear the most because our focus has been wrongfully on what we **don't** want, rather than what we **do** want. Fear can be described as 'False Evidence Appearing Real'. Often, the thing that we fear manifests not because it was inevitable, but because the fear gives it a focus that causes its manifestation.

Faith is the opposite of fear, and we are encouraged to walk by faith and not by sight. Walking by faith requires a level of courage as it requires that we act without certainty of future outcomes, and it is certainty that gives comfort and confidence. Faith is a muscle that must be developed to enable us to walk on the path we have been called to, and it is through faith that miracles occur and we are able to walk into the greatest destiny of our lives.

Satan is the opposite of all that God is and if God is love and we are made in the image and likeness of an infinite source, then we are love and fear is our enemy. Because we are an infinite creative force, fear is a destructive force and stagnates our very being, creativity and all that is good, such as peace and joy. On the other hand, fear generates everything that is bad and ultimately kills such as jealousy, hate, envy and strife.

All things exist already in the spiritual realm. I believe that fear stagnates us in the earthly realm but faith is the supernatural invisible bridge that connects us to the divine, which only exists in the supernatural. It is the substance that brings Thy kingdom on earth as it is in heaven.

Prayers

- ◊ *"I rebuke and renounce all words spoken against me, my family, my business and loved ones."* (Leviticus 19:17)

- ◊ *"I cancel all word curses and attacks from the enemy in Jesus' name."* (Isaiah 54:17)

- ◊ Lord, you said in John 10:10, that *"the thief does not come except to steal, and to kill, and to destroy. I have come that they may have life, and that they may have it more abundantly."* Therefore, I cancel all efforts of the enemy to steal, destroy and kill my life, health, family, business and finances.

- ◊ Matthew 18:18 says, *"Assuredly, I say to you, whatever you bind on earth will be bound in heaven, and whatever you loose on earth will be loosed in heaven."* Therefore, I bind the words of those who speak negativity over me and say 'Lord, I bind their words in Jesus' name.'

Ihu's Proclamations

- ◊ I bind the tongues, mouths, lips and voice boxes from speaking negative words, gossip, slander and anything that does not edify, exhort or build up.
- ◊ Each time you make a decision, ask yourself what is driving it: Fear or Love?
- ◊ My decisions are driven by love and not by fear.
- ◊ I act in faith, NOT fear.

Ihu's Reflections

- ◊ Take a moment to reflect on the key driving force behind most of your decision making. Ask yourself what is driving them. Is it coming from a place of fear or faith and love?
- ◊ Take a moment to reflect on your life. Do you observe any repetitive patterns or strange experiences that cannot be explained through the normal course of life's ups and downs?
- ◊ When you reflect on your wider experiences as a family, are there some strange or unpleasant phenomena that repeat in the family line?

Chapter Fifteen
Conclusion: The Purpose in the Passion and Pain

"And after you have suffered a little while, the God of all grace, who has called you to his eternal glory in Christ, will himself restore, confirm, strengthen, and establish you"

(1 Peter 5:10)

Treasure is not always wrapped up in finery. Treasure can often be found in the deepest, darkest, dirtiest and dingiest of places. Sometimes when we are in the painful pit of experiences in our lives, no one can see our pain or hear our cries. These are the times we must dig deep to pull out the beautiful jewels deposited within our souls that will make us who we were born to be.

In 2020, it finally started to make sense as to why I had to go through all my prior painful difficult experiences. It felt like a culmination point where I had finally passed the test and was attending my graduation! All that I had learned had come together; I had earned the certificate and started receiving honours for what I had been through thus far. Sealing the deal felt like a graduation.

If the previous years were the lean years, then these were definitely the fat years. The year started with a new lucrative contract where my pay more than doubled. My next contract was double that again! Further to that, my ministry grew and continues to grow.

The Building the Excellent Family summit, which started virtually in 2019, has grown to a 20-speaker summit, and in 2023 was held in person at London's iconic O2. My work with Cedarcube earned me a place in *The World Book of Greatness 2021*, as a 'Visionary of Greatness'. This has led me to win numerous awards and honours, including being one of the *New York Times* Top 30 Women Leaders to Look Out For in 2024 and *Global Woman Magazine* 100 Top Global Women Entrepreneurs to be Inspired 2024.

However, in December 2020, we were hit with devastation again. As mentioned, Chidi was hospitalised with Covid-19 from 23rd to 31st December. That was our very first Christmas apart since we got married. Chidi almost lost his life but even in that despair, there was a positive experience; he encountered God in a new way. On Christmas Eve night, while fighting for his life, he had an epiphany that all that ever mattered in life was unconditional love. He came to understand God, the infinite source, in a different way and this understanding aligned us more closely spiritually.

The following May, Chidi was elected as a local District Councillor, fulfilling his lifelong political dream and fulfilling a large part of his life purpose. Since then, he has received several non-executive directorships in prominent charity organisations, as well as an appointment as the deputy chair of the British Nigerian Councillors.

In addition, he was appointed in a new role which he thoroughly enjoys in programme management in the same council where he had served faithfully as a city inspector but had been repeatedly passed up for promotion. Does he often feel fatigue and physical pain from the hangover of Covid? Yes, he does, but his changed outlook and new lease of life is palpable. **This** is the power of purpose.

Why do we have to experience pain before we can make gain, you may ask? I have reflected on this question myself in quiet moments and the answer came to me; because God, our infinite source, wants to strip us down to our lowest common denominator. We were born into the world through pain and so it is with re-birth into our purpose. The first birth was when we were born physically, and the second birth was the day we discovered why we were born. We were born naked, but we were also born complete. God, the infinite source, had already planned and conceived the reason for our birthing and had made great efforts with all the details needed to deposit in us everything that we need to fulfil our mission and purpose.

If you reflect on your life, you will find that you have a unique skill, and ability that makes you who you are. Even identical twins are unique and never quite follow the same life path. There are different variations that make you unique; the gene pool of your parents and grandparents are unique, the part of the word you were born in, and even the constellation of the stars in the universe at the time of your birth are all unique. Your experience and the people you come across in life all make your path uniquely yours. This is why you must never take your gifts and talents for granted. Hone them and work on them diligently as if your life depends on them, because truly it does if you are to walk on the best pathway of life that the infinite source, your unique creator has mapped out for you.

God will require of us what we did with our time, treasure, and talents. Indeed *"For everyone to whom much is given, from him much will be required; and to whom much has been committed, of him they will ask the more."* (Luke 12:48)

Our treasure is not only our finances, but the resources He blessed us with, including our children and other people He sent to help us achieve our purpose such as destiny helpers. He would even require from us an account of those He put in our care to help who are unrelated to us.

God will also require of us an account of what we did with the ideas and opportunities He gave us. He will indeed require of us what we did with our talents, as illustrated in the parable of the talents in Matthew 25:14-30 where a master was travelling and gave his servants talents, five, two and one, respectively. The servant that received five talents traded with them and gained five more, likewise the servant that received two gained two more, but the one that received one buried his. When the master returned, they all gave account of what they did with their talents. He praised the first two servants saying, *"Well done, good and faithful servant; you have been faithful over a few things, I will make you ruler over many things. Enter into the joy of your lord."*

When it came to the last servant who received one talent, the servant accounted that he buried his talent because he was afraid knowing the master to be a hard man reaping where he had not sown and gathering where he had not scattered seed. The master surmised his judgement by saying:

"You wicked and lazy servant, you knew that I reap where I have not sown, and gather where I have not scattered seed. So you ought to have deposited my money with the bankers, and at my coming I would have received back my own with

interest. So take the talent from him, and give it to him who has ten talents.

"For to everyone who has, more will be given, and he will have abundance; but from him who does not have, even what he has will be taken away. And cast the unprofitable servant into the outer darkness. There will be weeping and gnashing of teeth."

Jesus came to depict the Kingdom of God to us and this parable paints the picture of how seriously God takes the gifts and talents He gave us. They are not to be misused or buried but to be developed diligently for the propagation of His Kingdom.

Just like a coconut is self-contained with all that is pertaining to life and nourishment, water, nutritious fruit and all within its outer husk and hard shell, God has also deposited in you everything that would make you and that you would need to fulfil your very own special life path.

Everything you need to make it in life is inside of you, nothing missing and nothing broken. However, like the proverbial coconut, you must be broken and poured out for what you carry in you to be useful to the world around you.

Similarly, you must also be tasted by others for them to enjoy the gift in you and to be nourished by the gift you have to give. Embrace then the whole process, the darkness, the breaking and the pain. Embrace also the joys of discovering your talents and gifts and benefiting from them as well as having them benefiting others. It is all part of the process of awakening that beauty that lies within you to fulfil your purpose, for in so doing, you will discover and awaken the source of your true divinity.

> "Arise, shine;
> For your light has come!
> And the glory of the LORD is risen upon you.
> For behold, the darkness shall cover the earth,
> And deep darkness the people;
> But the LORD will arise over you,
> And His glory will be seen upon you.
> The Gentiles shall come to your light,
> And kings to the brightness of your rising."
>
> (Isaiah 60:1)

References and Further Reading

DEDICATION:
Obi Nwa' Chinyere-Ezeh, *The Coup Menace: How to stop it and make Nigeria great*, CONC Resources of Africa Foundation, Lagos, Africa, 1986

CH 1:
Bob Proctor, Proctor Gallagher Institute
www.proctorgallagherinstitute.com

John C Maxwell
https://www.maxwellleadership.com

Roy T. Bennett, American Thought Leader
https://en.wikipedia.org/wiki/Robert_T._Bennett

Tekno – musician
https://en.wikipedia.org/wiki/Tekno_(musician)

CH 2:

Heather Picken, NLP coach
www.thinkific.com

Bessel van der Kolk, *The Body Keeps the Score*, Penguin, 2015

60% to 80% of primary care visits are due to stress: Nerurkar A, Bitton A, Davis RB, Phillips RS, Yeh G. 'When physicians counsel about stress: results of a national study', *JAMA Intern Med*, 2013 Jan 14; 173(1):76-7. doi: 10.1001/2013.jamainternmed.480. PMID: 23403892; PMCID: PMC4286362.

Dr Elizabeth Scott: How to Handle a Stress-Related Psychosomatic Response, www.verywellmind.com)

'Dzigbordi K Dosoo: The multi-passionate phenomenon', *The Business & Financial Times*, www.thebftonline.com, 4 December 2017.

Marie Forleo
http://www.marieforleo.com

Shannon Kaiser, '3 Unexpected Ways to Find Your Life Purpose', *HuffPost Life*, 19 April 2014

Cedarcube
www.cedarcube.com

Dr Kinga Mnich, 'What is a multi-passionate person?', https://kingamnich.com/

Wai-Yee Schmidt
https://kingsandwealth.com/about-us/

Ihu's clothing brand, I.Kollection
https://i-kollection.com

Mel Robbins, *The 5 Second Rule*, Savio Republic, 2017.

James Clear, *Atomic Habits*, Random House Business, 2018.

Gary Keller & Jay Papasan, *The One Thing*, John Murray One, 2014.

Chris Weller, 'Bill Gates and Steve Jobs raised their kids tech-free – and it should've been a red flag, *The Independent*, 24 October 2017.

Nick Bilton, 'Steve Jobs Was a Low-Tech Parent', *New York Times*, https://www.nytimes.com/2014/09/11/fashion/steve-jobs-apple-was-a-low-tech-parent.html?_r=0

Dr Michelle Anthony, 'Creative Development in 3-5 Year Olds', https://www.scholastic.com/parents/family-life/creativity-and-critical-thinking/development-milestones/creative-development-3-5-year-olds.html

CH 4:

Reading the Past with Dr Kat
https://www.youtube.com/@ReadingthePast

Annie Strauch of Performance Medicine
https://performancemedicine.com.au/practitioners/annie-strauch-2/

Ogilvy & Mather
https://www.ogilvy.com

Marie Diamond
https://www.mariediamond.com

CH 5:

Cognitive Science Journal
https://onlinelibrary.wiley.com/journal/15516709

Journal of Neurology Research Reviews
https://www.onlinescientificresearch.com/journal-of-neurology-research-reviews-reports-home-jnrrr.php

Gandra Sridhar Rao, Neelkanth M. Pujari, Rupali Yadav, Amrita Shukla, *Textbook Of Medical Physiology And Human Anatomy*, AGPH Books, 2023

Daniel Dennett, *Consciousness Explained*, Penguin, 1993

Left vs Right Brain: what's the Difference: https://www.webmd.com/brain/the-difference-between-the-left-and-right-brain

CH 6:

The Seven Mountains of Influence/The Seven Mountains of Culture
https://en.wikipedia.org/wiki/Seven_Mountain_Mandate

Lance Wallnau and Bill Johnson, *Invading Babylon: The 7 Mountain Mandate*, Destiny Image, 2016

CH 8:

https://praypedia.com/prayer/timemanagement.html

CH 9:

Hannah Sampson, 'Hotel Bibles are still a thing, but probably not for much longer', *The Washington Post*, February 2020

https://www.crosswalk.com/faith/prayer/10-prayers-that-will-transform-your-finances.html

CH 12:

Aisha Dabi, 'Women are the key to economic development in third-world countries', https://www.kcl.ac.uk/news/women-are-the-key-to-economic-development-in-third-world-countries, 28 August, 1019

CH 13:

Worthman CM, Tomlinson M, Rotheram-Borus MJ, 'When can parents most influence their child's development? Expert knowledge and perceived local realities, *Soc Sci Med.* 2016 Apr;154:62-9. doi: 10.1016/j.socscimed.2016.02.040. Epub 2016 Feb 26. PMID: 26945544; PMCID: PMC4826572.

The Best Start for Life
https://assets.publishing.service.gov.uk/media/605c5e61d3bf7f2f0d94183a/The_best_start_for_life_a_vision_for_the_1_001_critical_days.pdf

Special Thanks

In the course of writing this book, I called for interviews to explore people's personal experiences of passion and pain and how it had shaped their lives, helping to achieve their purpose. Some of these stories made it to the book, but some didn't.

All the same, I would like to thank all the women who gave generously of their time and shared their deeply personal stories of highs and low.

These phenomenal women are: Brenda Dempsey, Donia Youssef, Heather Picken, Jennifer Crowe, Michelle Watson, Patricia Ralijemisa, Sabrina Ben Salmi, Uju Maduforo and Kicki Pallin.

Thank you all for trusting me to share your stories. Your unique journeys are a testament of the strength and resilience of the human spirit and the ability to push through it all to fulfil life's journey.

About the Author

Ihuaku Patricia Nweke is a social entrepreneur, creative, author and international speaker. She is the founder of Cedarcube, a social enterprise focused on family restoration.

In October 2018, Cedarcube established the Behind the Mask project, which has helped a number of women and families affected by domestic abuse, providing them with counselling and therapy, as well as educational and financial support, particularly during the Covid-19 pandemic.

In 2019, Cedarcube was shortlisted out of over 20,000 organisations nationwide for the National Diversity Awards. Cedarcube has won several awards, such as the London Live Wire Prestige Awards for Relationship Counselling Service

2019. Ihuaku was also a finalist in the Humanitarian of the Year Award for the Women 4 Africa Awards.

Through her work with Cedarcube, Ihuaku represents her local council, Epping Forest District Council, as a community champion.

Ihuaku has always had a creative flair and in July 2008, she pursued her creative passions in earnest, undertaking training in fashion and design and starting her own jewellery and fashion line, I.Kollection. Since then, I.Kollection fashion has featured in *Vogue*, African Fashion Week London (AFWL), Fashion Finest London Fashion Week, and projects with the Common Wealth Fashion Council. I.Kollection had also won several awards, such as Ethnic Minority Business of the Year with the International Trade Council.

Ihuaku is a Chartered Procurement professional (MCIPS) and for 20 years, she has been a consultant in procurement to several UK public sector organisations such as Department of Food and Rural Affairs, the NHS, the Ministry of Justice and Transport for London.

She is an Amazon bestselling author and has been a speaker at several international forums, including the Women's Economic Forum. In 2015, she was conferred with the Chieftain title of Ola Edo (Gold) of Ndumeze Kingdom. Ihuaku is currently an official CSW68 UK Delegate to the United Nations for the status on women and girls. She has also recently been featured in the *New York Times* Top 30 Women Leaders to Watch in 2024 and the Top 100 Top 100 Entrepreneurial Women 2024.

Ihuaku is married to Chidiebere Nweke and they are blessed with three bright and energetic boys.

How to contact Ihuaku

www.ihuakupnweke.com

hello@ihuakupnweke.com

https://linktr.ee/ihuakupnweke